TV Dinners

IN SEARCH OF EXCITING HOME COOKING

HUGH FEARNLEY-WHITTINGSTALL

WITH HATTIE ELLIS

BOXTREE

IN ASSOCIATION WITH CHANNEL FOUR TELEVISION CORPORATION

DEDICATION

This book is dedicated to the 13 cooks featured,
who were brave enough to let the cameras into their kitchens –
not to mention having their friends round to dinner.

TV Dinners was produced for
Channel Four Television by
Ricochet Films Limited

First published in Great Britain in 1996 by Boxtree Limited

Photographs by Stuart Wood, except those on pp. 11, 14, 50, 82, 105, 106, 111, 114, 122, 139,141, 142, 147 which are by Robin Chanda, and those on pp. 129, 131, 134 which are by Nicky Dowee

1 2 3 4 5 6 7 8 9 10

Designed by DW Design
Printed and bound in the UK by Bath Press, Colour Books for

Boxtree Limited
Broadwall House
21 Broadwall
London SE1 9PL

A CIP catalogue entry for this book is available from the British Library

ISBN 0 7522 1064 5

Front jacket photograph by Robin Broadbent
Back jacket photographs by Robin Chanda (top) and Stuart Wood (below)

CONTENTS

INTRODUCTION

I don't suppose anyone knows when the first dinner party was given. But I like to imagine that maybe one day, in some well-appointed executive cave, our ancestors, Mr and Mrs Nog and family, were enjoying a lightly grilled haunch of mammoth, nice and pink in the middle, when they heard a bash on the front rock: their neighbours, the Egs, coming once again to try and steal their supper.

For once, instead of rushing to beat off the potential food thieves with sticks and clubs, Mr Nog sized up the large pile of meat in front of him, scratched his head for a moment, and called out to the Egs, 'Come on in! Actually, we've got a little more mammoth than we can manage ourselves. It would be so nice if you could join us. . . '

And I dare say, as the Egs wandered home, bellies sated with flesh, Mr Eg might have been heard to mutter, 'I suppose we'll have to ask them back now.'

Since then, in every culture, the process of sharing food with family and friends has been, and will surely continue to be, one of the essential bonding agents of the social fabric. Today and every day, all over the world, people will be crossing the street, field, village or town to meet and eat at the homes of their good friends.

But dinner parties are not straightforward. Over time, a highly complex set of unwritten rules has evolved to help the smooth running of these more or less formal occasions: social norms, or what we sometimes call 'etiquette'. These conventions will differ radically, of course, depending on where you are – and not just between nations and classes, but from one end of the street to the other. This is one of the things that makes going out to dinner so fascinating: no two hosts entertain in quite the same way.

But whether our neighbours arrive with a six-pack, the port is passed to the left, or we offer the sheep's eyes first to the most honoured guest, we are all engaged in the same basic process: sharing food with our friends, in exchange for the pleasure of their company. It's something we have all done, and will all do again.

Given its social history and universality, it seems strange that television has never before tackled the dinner party head on. *TV Dinners* wasn't my idea. But when the producer, Nick Powell of Ricochet Films, called me about it, my immediate response was, 'I wish I'd thought of that.' From its earliest days, television has had cooking programmes, and home cooks have been bombarded with ideas from self-appointed 'experts' on home entertaining, telling us how to do it. But how much more interesting to find out how people actually are doing it.

Recently we have seen a great deal of exciting cooking on the television, executed by slick professional cooks who have stepped out of their steel and tile kitchens and into the frame of the magic rectangle. I am not about to knock either their talents or their influence – indeed, many of the home cooks in our series are avid fans of the TV chefs, and take great inspiration from their books and programmes. But the state of the nation's culinary art is not to be judged by what star chefs are doing first in their restaurants and then on television. The truth about British cooking is to be found in the kitchens and dining rooms of real people's homes. What we set out to discover in *TV Dinners* was what dishes and styles of cooking, both new and old, exotic and home-grown, elaborate and simple, were filtering through the fine-meshed sieve of people's culinary consciousnesses and ending up on the table when friends came round for dinner. Or to put it another way, we wanted to get to the nub of our grub.

What we found on our quest was not just an abundance of exciting home cooking, but confirmation that our food culture is in the throws of a revolution. The British home kitchen has become a hot-bed of creativity, in which we are gleaning inspiration and ideas from all over world, to produce a heady mixture of dishes that are by turns original, classic, surprising, outrageous and, in all cases, bursting with freshness and flavour. What you will find on these pages are clear instructions for the preparation of some of the very best dishes being cooked in Britain today. All the recipes have been tested by real home cooks in their own kitchens. If they can do it, so can you.

But there is more to giving dinner parties than putting food on the table. Entertaining means many different things to different people. For some, it provides an opportunity to show off their wealth and social status. For others, it is an occasion for high jinx, revelry and bawdiness. Some think formality and social graces important, while others take casualness to an art form. Some find the whole process highly stressful, others find it deeply therapeutic. During the course of filming *TV Dinners*, our various hosts revealed, either directly or indirectly, a whole range of feelings and motives behind the style and content of the meals they cook for friends.

Such nuances are perhaps more easily expressed through television than in print. Nevertheless I have, in the introductions to each chapter, and to some of the recipes, tried to recall a little flavour of the host's character, a sense of their style, their homes, and their philosophy of entertaining. For those who have seen the series these will, I hope, ring bells of recognition. And for those who haven't, they will at least put the food in the context of a personality and an occasion.

Making the series had many pleasures for me, not all of them connected directly with my stomach. I have travelled all over the country, got a bit of fishing in, and exercised my penchant for being a nosey parker in all kinds of interesting places. Without a doubt, however, the greatest pleasure has been to meet, share food, and talk about life with a dozen (a baker's dozen, appropriately enough) warm, talented, generous and genuinely hospitable hosts. On behalf of myself and the whole *TV Dinners* crew, I would like to thank them all for having us.

Hugh Fearnley-Whittingstall
July 1996

A FAMILY AFFAIR

Michael Massarella

MENU

Grilled rack of lamb with pepper and herb marinade
Grilled lettuce and Gorgonzola
Griglio misto with seasoned brown butter
Grilled fennel with shaved Parmesan
Pizza
Grilled polenta with wild mushrooms and red onions
Broccoli and chicken salad with polenta croûtons

Fritelle
Sweet white wine granita with mixed berries

The main difference between professional chefs and amateur cooks is not, on the evidence of this series at least, their greater understanding of, or enthusiasm for, food. These are qualities which many of our home cooks have in spades. It is, I suspect, more to do with speed and confidence under pressure.

But out of all our cooks, Michael, unusually, had as much confidence and energy in the kitchen as any professional, which I imagine is either a cause, or an effect, of the scale on which he likes to entertain – he hardly ever cooks for less than twenty. It also makes him an exhilarating person to cook with – provided you can keep up! He quickly lost patience with the sight of me languorously kneeding the dough for his fritelle. 'Come on, Hugh!' he said, grabbing it from me. 'You don't have to mess about with this stuff' – as he beat and pummelled it into submission.

Michael also has what I call 'cook's luck' – that enviable knack for getting things right, without much recourse to books, weights or measures. 'I can't be doing with all this weighing business,' he told me, as he shook the polenta straight from the bag into the pan of boiling water, 'and I seem to get away with it most of the time.'

A Yorkshireman of Italian descent, the Italian blood holds sway in the kitchen. His style of his cooking, which is very rustic, is reinforced by numerous Italian holidays, where Michael, who is the only one of four brothers to have learned the language, prises culinary secrets from the many friends he has made there. 'I'm a third-generation Yorkshireman,' he says, 'and proud enough of that. But whenever I get off a plane in Italy, I feel like I've come home.'

He also has the host's advantage of a large house and beautiful garden. With the help of his girlfriend Karen, Michael has created 'a little corner of Tuscany' – just outside Doncaster. For summer entertaining they have converted an outbuilding into a

Tuscan–style covered veranda. In it he has built by hand, as well as a barbecue, the ultimate gesture to Italian country cooking: his very own wood-fired brick pizza oven. 'It was a real labour of love,' he told me proudly, running his hand across the brickwork, 'built from memory. So the fact that it actually works is maybe a bit fortunate.' More cook's luck, no doubt.

As lunchtime drew nearer, astonishing amounts of food began to accumulate in the kitchen: plates of salamis and hams, another of grilled courgettes, great bowls of green salad, a tray of shellfish *spedieno* (kebabs), and two whole racks of lamb, marinated in oil and herbs and destined for the barbecue.

But this wasn't a solo effort. Michael is no slouch when it comes to delegation, and Karen and his daughter Daniella had been quietly busy behind the scenes. 'He's very good at getting us to do things,' Daniella told me, as she turned the courgettes on the griddle, 'and quite bossy sometimes.'

As the guests arrive, Michael likes to get them all involved – taking turns to tend the barbecue, toss a salad or bake a pizza. When I was assigned to pizza-oven duty I got distracted in football talk with Daniella and her friend Tizzy, and burned my pizza to a crisp. 'There's no Italian blood in you,' said Michael. 'No,' I had to admit. 'It's pure King Alfred.'

All the barbecue recipes below can also be cooked indoors, ideally on a cast-iron grill pan (the kind with raised ridges), but also under a conventional eye-level grill.

Grilled Rack of Lamb with Pepper and Herb Marinade

Cooking meat on the bone maximizes flavour, and cooking a whole rack of lamb on a barbecue adds a touch of glamour to outdoor eating. Michael cooked four racks of lamb for his twenty or so guests, two on the barbecue and two in the wood-fired pizza oven (they were, if anything, even more delicious).

Two racks of lamb should serve eight–ten as part of a barbecue or buffet. Halve the quantities for the marinade for just one rack of lamb.

290 ml/½ pint olive oil

4 tbspn balsamic vinegar

360 ml/12 fl oz red wine

3 handfuls of fresh chopped herbs, such as rosemary, sage and parsley

4 cloves of garlic, finely chopped

salt and freshly ground black pepper

2 whole racks of lamb, trimmed by your butcher so the cutlets split away easily

1. Mix together the olive oil, balsamic vinegar, red wine, two handfuls of herbs, the garlic, salt and plenty of pepper. Taste and adjust flavours if necessary.
2. Cover the racks of lamb with the marinade and refrigerate for several hours or overnight, turning a few times.
3. When the time arrives to cook, remove the lamb from marinade and place on an oiled grill rack over a medium heat on the barbeque or on an oiled griddle pan on a hob.
4. Grilling time will depend on how you like your meat cooked and how close your grill is to the fire. Michael takes about 12-15 minutes quite close to the fire for meat that is nicely charred on the outside and very pink in the middle. Keep turning the meat and basting it with the marinade during cooking.
5. Split the lamb cutlets apart with a large knife or a cleaver. Put on a serving plate with more freshly ground black pepper and the rest of the chopped herbs.
6. If some people like their meat more well done, you can easily put individual cutlets back on the barbecue for a few extra minutes.
7. Put the spare marinade in a pan on the barbecue or hob and bubble to reduce it to a tasty gravy to serve with the cutlets.

Griglio Misto ▶

Grilled Lettuce and Gorgonzola

I'd had grilled radicchio before, but grilled green lettuces were a revelation. Michael serves this dish with chilled Lambrusco, a slightly sparkling Italian red wine. If you don't like blue cheese, goat's cheese or Taleggio would be a good substitute. Good fruity olive oil is essential.

serves six as a starter or as part of a barbecue or buffet

- *150 ml/¼ pint olive oil*
- *salt and freshly ground black pepper*
- *6 little gem lettuces or 2 tightly packed cos lettuces*
- *250 g/9 oz Gorgonzola or Dolcelatte cheese*
- *2 lemons, quartered*

1. Mix the olive oil, salt and pepper in a shallow dish.
2. Cut the little gems in half (or the cos into three) lengthways, leaving the stem intact to stop the leaves breaking away.
3. Coat the lettuce well in the seasoned oil, using a brush or spoon.
4. Place the lettuce, cut side down, on the oiled grill rack of a barbecue or on an oiled cast-iron grill pan on a hob. Cook over a medium heat for 4-5 minutes, depending on size. Turn and baste with more oil two or three times during cooking. The lettuces are ready when they look slightly wilted, with burn marks from the grill, and the thick stems are just becoming tender.
5. Arrange the lettuce pieces on a large platter (or two halves of little gem/one piece of cos per person on individual plates). Crumble over the cheese and drizzle with a good fruity olive oil.
6. If convenient, put the platter in a medium oven for just a couple of minutes, to encourage the cheese to melt and brown on top.
7. Serve with bread, big juicy lemon wedges and a glass of good red wine.

Note: *Use any of the seasoned olive oil left over to baste other food on the barbecue.*

Griglio Misto

Michael's favourite dish when visiting Italy is fritto misto, platters of freshly caught fish and seafood, battered and deep-fried. His barbecue version uses unbattered squid, prawns, scallops and monkfish, threaded on to wooden skewers and served simply with plenty of lemon wedges.

serves six as a starter or as part of a barbecue or buffet

- *500 g/1 lb 2 oz monkfish tails*
- *450 g/1 lb fresh whole squid bodies, cleaned*
- *12 large prawns (Mediterranean, Tiger or Dublin Bay prawns)*
- *12 large fresh scallops (frozen are not recommended)*

1. Soak six wooden skewers in warm water for a few hours, to stop them burning on the barbecue.
2. Cut the monkfish meat off the tail bone and slice into skewerable chunks, and slice the squid bodies into skewerable lengths. Ideally, you want twelve pieces of each in all.
3. Thread the fish and shellfish on to the skewers, about two pieces of each type of fish on each skewer.
4. Mix the garlic and chilli with the olive oil. Further season the oil with salt and pepper. Brush the skewered fish generously with this seasoned oil, leaving little pieces of chilli and garlic on the fish.

2 large cloves of garlic, finely chopped

1 small fresh red chilli, seeded and finely chopped

2 tbspn olive oil

salt and freshly ground black pepper

5. Place the skewers of fish on an oiled rack over a hot barbecue (or on a tin tray under an eye-level grill). Cook for 5-10 minutes according to the heat of your barbecue. Turn and baste with extra olive oil and/or seasoned browned butter (recipe follows), as required.
6. Serve with lemon wedges and/or seasoned browned butter.

Seasoned Browned Butter

A useful barbecue or grill baste, especially for fish (try fresh sardines) and chicken.

450 g/1 lb unsalted butter

juice of 2 lemons

salt and freshly ground black pepper

Tabasco sauce

flat leaf parsley

1. Melt the butter until it starts to froth and brown and has a rich nutty smell. Take care it does not burn.
2. Stir in the lemon juice to taste. Season with salt, pepper and Tabasco to taste.
3. Use the browned butter to baste fish (or chicken) while cooking. Pour any that is left at the end of cooking over the fish, then sprinkle with freshly chopped parsley.

Grilled Fennel with Shaved Parmesan

The distinctive flavour of fennel is not to everybody's taste although it is very much to mine. The barbecue, which caramelizes the sugars and produces those delectable zebra stripes, is a fine way to make converts.

serves six as part of a barbecue or buffet

6 bulbs of fennel

olive oil

salt and freshly ground black pepper

Parmesan cheese

1. Trim the fennel bulbs, cutting off the outermost layers if they are not completely fresh. Cut each bulb in half downwards, keeping the stem intact, and, if the bulbs are large, in half again, to make quarters.
2. Blanch the fennel in plenty of boiling salted water for just 2-3 minutes so they are slightly tenderized but still quite crunchy. Drain and, when cool, pat dry.
3. Brush each piece of fennel with olive oil and season well with salt and pepper. Place on a grill rack over the barbecue or on a hot cast-iron grill pan. Turn and baste as required until nicely browned on all sides. Allow to cool.
4. To make Parmesan shavings take a block of Parmesan, trimmed of rind, and a potato peeler, and 'peel' thin shavings of the cheese.
5. Scatter the Parmesan shavings over the fennel, pour over an extra drizzle of olive oil, give it a few twists of black pepper and serve at once.

Pizza

Grilled lettuce and Gorgonzola ▲

Food-processor Pizza Base

Michael says that while purists will use their hands to make this pizza dough, he wants to get eating as soon as possible and so uses a food processor. He likes pizza to have a really thin base and serves it as a tasty form of bread as part of a barbecue or buffet. Custom-made pizza tins with holes in the bottom, to help crisp up the base, are available at good kitchen shops.

enough for two large or four small pizza bases

450 g/1 lb strong white bread flour

1 tspn salt

½ tspn sugar

1. Sift the flour and put it into the food processor bowl with the salt, sugar and yeast.
2. Switch the food processor to maximum speed. Add a couple of tablespoons of the oil down the tube and half the water in a steady stream. The mixture should resemble breadcrumbs.
3. Add the rest of the water, a drop at a time, until the mixture forms a slightly sticky dough ball. If you have added too much water add a little more flour and vice versa.
4. Transfer to a floured surface and knead for a couple of minutes until smooth.

½ to ¾ of a 7 g/¼ oz sachet of instant yeast

approximately 120 ml/4 fl oz good olive oil

360 ml/12 fl oz warm water

5 Brush a bowl with some olive oil. Shape the dough into a ball, brush with olive oil and place in the bowl. Cover with a cloth and put in a warm place until it doubles in size (approximately 1-1½ hours).
6 Preheat the oven to 230°C/450°F/Gas mark 8.
7 Take the dough out of the bowl. Knock it down with your fists and split it into two or four balls, depending on the size of your pizza tins.
8 On a well-floured surface, flatten the balls out into approximately 25 cm/10 in rounds, either by hand or using a rolling pin.
9 Put on to pizza trays or baking trays and brush with olive oil. Add your topping (see below) and bake in the middle of the preheated oven for 10-15 minutes.
10 Finish the cooked pizza with more olive oil and fresh herbs.

Tomato Sauce for Pizza Bases

This basic tomato sauce, rich and thick, should be spread sparingly on a fresh pizza base, which can then be topped with mozzarella and any number of extra ingredients.

2 tbspn olive oil

1 clove of garlic, chopped

1 large tin (800 g/1 lb 10 oz) peeled plum tomatoes

salt and black pepper

1 Heat the olive oil in a heavy frying pan and throw in the garlic.
2 Just as the garlic starts to take colour, add the tomatoes. Bring to the boil, and simmer, stirring regularly to make sure the sauce doesn't catch on the bottom of the pan, until reduced to a thick pulpy sauce. Then (and only then) season to taste with salt and pepper.

Assembly

1 Spread each pizza base with a thin layer of tomato sauce, scatter with torn-up slices of mozzarella and top with any of the following: other cheeses such as goat's cheese or Taleggio • pepperoni sausages• pancetta or Parma ham • artichoke hearts • olives • sautéed mushrooms• anchovies • capers • grilled courgette slices • and just about anything else.

Pizza Bianca

This simplest of all pizzas is distinctive for its lack of tomato. It can be served as a snack with drinks or instead of bread as a side dish at a barbecue, as Michael does.

2 large or 4 small pizza bases

olive oil

250 g/9 oz mozzarella cheese

a few sprigs dried rosemary

salt and black pepper

1 Brush the pizza bases with olive oil.
2 Slice the mozzarella and then tear it into small pieces. Scatter roughly over the pizza bases.
3 Sprinkle the dried rosemary over the cheese, then season with salt and pepper.
4 Bake in the preheated oven as above.

Grilled Polenta with Wild Mushrooms and Red Onions

Polenta is a supremely versatile staple food in Italy, simple but much loved. Michael's friend Letitzia Bergomi serves it 'wet' – straight from the saucepan – with a fresh boiling sausage and plenty of butter and Parmesan. And every time she mounds up a plate, her husband Adolpho's eyes light up. Originally a humble dish, polenta now features on menus in top restaurants all over the world. Michael admits it took him some time to take to polenta, but now he is addicted to its versatility and eats it hot and cold, in snacks, starters and main courses, spread with all sorts of toppings, from eggs to pesto to this red onion, mushroom and mozzarella one. An instant variety available at some supermarkets cooks in just a few minutes and thus takes the heavy elbow work out of the job.

serves six or eight as part of a buffet

450 g/1 lb bag of real or instant polenta

4 red onions, thinly sliced

1 tbspn oil

15 g/½ oz butter

450 g/1 lb mushrooms (wild or a mixture of wild and cultivated), peeled or washed and sliced

a couple of handfuls of fresh herbs, such as oregano, parsley and basil, finely chopped

125 g/4 oz mozzarella

1. In a large pan, bring 2 litres/3½ pints of salted water up to the boil, then lower the heat so it is gently simmering. Pour in the polenta in a steady thin stream, stirring all the time with a wooden spoon. The polenta will start to thicken and bubble. To avoid the dreaded lumps, you must stir all the time in the same direction. If lumps should appear, don't panic – a little vigorous work with a balloon whisk should get rid of them. When the polenta starts to stiffen and pull away from the pan sides (after 25-35 minutes) it is ready.
2. When cooked, pour the polenta into a shallow rectangular dish or tray and spread with a spatula to a depth of about 2–3 cm/1-1¼ in. Leave to go cold.
3. Fry the sliced red onions in a pan with oil and butter until soft but not over-browned. Add the mushrooms and continue cooking until their juices have been released and sweated off. Set aside.
4. Cut the cold polenta into shapes (squares, circles, rectangles, etc.), larger or smaller, depending on whether you are serving them as canapés, starters or a main course.
5. Top each piece of polenta with the onion and mushroom mixture. Sprinkle with herbs. Place a little piece of mozzarella cheese on top and flash under the grill or place in a hot oven (220°C/425°F/Gas mark 7) until brown and bubbling.
6. Serve at once, but warn the greedy not to burn their mouths.

Broccoli and Chicken Salad with Polenta Croûtons

Michael is a very natural cook, much given to last-minute improvisations. During a break in filming he knocked up this excellent salad with a few leftovers and a tin of anchovies. Not only did it taste good, but it also looked quite beautiful!

serves four as a starter, six as part of a buffet

250 g/8 oz broccoli

1 or 2 chicken breasts, or leftover chicken

polenta scraps

1 small tin of anchovies

250 g/8 oz cooked penne or other cooked pasta shapes

3 tbspn best olive oil

1 dsstspn balsamic vinegar

salt and freshly ground black pepper

1. Blanch the broccoli for just two or three minutes in salted boiling water – it should still be nice and crunchy – rinse in cold water to keep the colour fresh, then leave to drain in a colander. Cut into bite-size florets.
2. Grill or barbecue the chicken breasts until done, then cut into strips.
3. Chop the polenta scraps into little nuggets, then grill or fry until nice and crispy.
4. Drain the anchovies and roughly chop.
5. In a large salad bowl, toss the pasta with the olive oil, vinegar, broccoli, anchovies, chicken and salt and pepper. Sprinkle the crispy polenta over the top and serve.

Fritelle/Crispelle

These little fried pastries are a must in Italy at carnival time, or any celebration, though whichever part of the country you are in they have a different name. Michael's sister-in-law, Franca, who comes from Sardinia, calls them chiacchere della nonna, which means 'Granny's gossip'. Whatever they are called, making them is about the most fun you can have in the kitchen – until you come to eat them, that is.

serves five–six people (though Michael and I could probably eat the lot)

170 g/6 oz good Italian flour 00 grade (or plain cake flour)

½ tspn baking powder

1½ tbspn caster sugar

pinch of salt

3 tbspn liqueur (Michael uses grappa or white rum)

1 large egg yolk

1. Sieve the flour, baking powder, sugar and salt on to the work surface, forming a mound, and make a well in the middle.
2. Into this well, put the liqueur, egg yolk, milk and butter and mix with your hands until it comes together into a dough. Knead fast and hard until it is smooth and elastic. If it feels unworkably hard, add some extra milk or if it becomes too sticky to handle, add some extra flour.
3. Form the dough into a ball. Cover with clingfilm and leave at room temperature for 1-2 hours.
4. Roll out the dough on a floured surface. The thinner the dough, the better the frittelle. Michael rolls it on a plastic tablecloth until he can see the pattern through the dough.
5. Cut the dough into lasagne-sized rectangles, then into strips 2–3 cm/1–1¼ in wide

2 tbspn semi-skimmed milk

30 g/1 oz unsalted butter

sunflower oil for deep-frying

icing sugar for dusting

and 6–8 cm/2½–3 in long. Put a 2 cm/1 in slash down the middle of each piece and pass one end through, shaking it out gently to get a bow shape.

6 Using a deep pan (or, for safe frying in the presence of children, a safety deep-fat fryer), heat a few centimetres of sunflower oil until it is very hot. Fry the bows in small batches until pale golden and puffed up. This takes only 30 seconds or so, and they will require one turn to be evenly cooked. The oil must be hot, but watch out that the biscuits do not burn.
7 Remove the fritelle from the oil and drain on kitchen paper. Repeat until all the biscuits are cooked.
8 Pile on a large platter, sprinkling each layer with icing sugar and eat hot or cold. They can be served with a granita or sorbet, or with coffee and grappa at the end of a meal. They are best eaten within a few hours. Don't try and keep until the following day (not that you'd want to).

Sweet White Wine Granita with Mixed Berries

This refreshing ice is really easy to make using any sweet or dessert wine and any berries. The advantage of a granita over a sorbet is that you don't have to interrupt the freezing process with endless whisking – the mixture is allowed to freeze solid, then texture is created by scraping into crystals with a fork.

serves four–six

360 ml/12 fl oz sweet white wine

45 g/1½ oz granulated sugar

120 ml/4 fl oz water

225 g/8 oz mixed summer berries – strawberries, raspberries, redcurrants, blackberries, etc.

juice of a ½ lemon

2 cinnamon sticks

150 ml/¼ pint whipping cream, softly whipped optional

1 Boil the wine, sugar and water, stirring occasionally until the sugar has dissolved and you have a syrupy consistency.
2 Set aside a few of the best berries for decoration. In a mixing bowl, with a wooden spoon (not metal) crush the rest of the berries so that they release their juices. Add these to the pan with the lemon juice and two cinnamon sticks and simmer for several more minutes.
3 Strain the mixture through a fine sieve into a shallow glass baking dish or plastic dish. Cover with clingfilm and put in freezer for three–four hours, or overnight, until frozen solid.
4 Chill a deep serving glass for each person in the freezer for a couple of hours. When you take them out they will have a frosted appearance.
5 Just before you want to eat, fork the surface granita into soft, snowy crystals.
6 Place some berries each glass. Top with granita and then the whipped cream, if you are using. Add more berries and serve at once with frittelle or biscotti.

Sweet white wine granita with mixed berries, with fritelle in the background ▶

THE FRENCH CONNECTION

Selina Snow

MENU

Globe artichokes with garlic butter

Sea bass with fennel, lemon and thyme
Saffron and lemon mayonnaise
Warm potato and olive salad

Prune and Armagnac tart

Selina Snow is an artist by trade and a cook by nature. The two activities are so intertwined in her life that sometimes even she doesn't know where one ends and the other begins. 'If I reach a block in my painting,' she told me, 'I instinctively head for the kitchen. And when I've made something, and maybe eaten it, I come back into the studio and find that everything's flowing again. I don't know how it works, but it always does.'

Selina owes her artist's instincts, and to some extent her love of food, to her father, painter and theatrical designer Peter Snow. 'When I was six, he decided to send me to the French Lycée in London, and every so often we would take the ferry to Boulogne to get the books I needed. I can't really remember the books but I remember spending a lot of time wandering around the food market, buying wine and visiting cake shops. I'm convinced the main reason he wanted me to learn French was so I could help him with the food shopping.'

Selina wanted to cook a special sixty-ninth birthday dinner for Peter and it was to Boulogne that she returned, with Peter and myself in tow, to acquire the very best ingredients. In particular, she was on a fish mission. She had recently overcome her 'fear of fish' (though she still didn't much like gutting them) and had been getting to grips with fish cookery. She also wanted to steer Peter, a dedicated Dover sole man, towards new and more unusual varieties. The Boulogne fish market is not exactly picturesque, but the fishwives (who are literally, in most cases, the wives of fishermen) certainly know their fish. In the end we came away from the quay with some beautiful sea bass, at about 350-400g/12-14 oz perfect for one person, and so fresh they were practically winking at us.

As Peter went off for a quiet cake, and Selina and I wandered among the overflowing colours of the market, it soon became clear that Selina's artistic alliance with food is not confined to the kitchen. If cooking is her therapy, then shopping is her inspiration. She appraises raw ingredients with her hands, her eyes, and – when she sees something she really likes – with her camera. She has albums full of photographs of the food she has seen, touched, smelt and eaten, taken in markets, restaurants, at home and at the homes of her friends. 'People who invite me to dinner think it's odd enough when I get my camera out,' she says, 'but when I start taking pictures of the food they've cooked, and not of them, they think I'm really loopy.' Why does she do this? 'Very occasionally a particular photograph inspires a particular picture, but altogether these pictures are my accumulative inspiration, and also a kind of diary. I can remember far more about an evening – who was there, what happened, and what was said – from a picture of the food we ate than I ever would from a picture of the people.'

While we were filming in Boulogne and cooking in Selina's Kensington flat, I noticed that her relationship with food is not unlike her relationship with her father – intense but not tense, playful but deep, and, in the final analysis, rather touching and tender.

Anyone for whom she cooks is going to feel very special and, at the end of it all, very very full!

Caper and Anchovy Toasts

Selina likes to serve these as snacks with drinks, but topped with a couple of cooked asparagus spears or a strip of toasted red or yellow pepper they are easily elevated to starter status. Adapted from a recipe by Marie-Pierre Moine.

serves six

1 small tin of anchovies in oil

4 tbspn capers

1–2 tbspn olive oil

12 slices of brioche or soda bread

optional

cooked asparagus tips, 12 small or 6 large, halved

1 red or yellow pepper, grilled, skinned and cut into thin strips

1. Drain the anchovies from their oil. Mix the capers and anchovies in a food processor, or chop together with a large knife.
2. Add enough olive oil to achieve a spreadable consistency.
3. Toast the brioche or bread and, while the slices are still warm, spread with a generous amount of paste.
4. If using, top with asparagus tips or slices of grilled pepper.
5. Serve straight away, with more olive oil drizzled on top.

Toasted Almonds

The simplest of drinks nibbles, but freshly toasted and still warm they are unbeatable.

1 handful of whole unblanched almonds (i.e. skins still on) per person

Maldon sea-salt flakes

1. Heat the oven to 190°C/375°F/Gas mark 5.
2. Put the almonds on a roasting tray. Scatter with the sea-salt flakes, bearing in mind that they are stronger than ordinary salt.
3. Toast for 6 or 7 minutes, shaking the tray once or twice and keeping an eye on that nuts to see that they do not burn.
4. Serve warm – but remember to warn your guests if they are still piping hot!

Sea bass with fennel, lemon and thyme, ready for the oven ▶

SPECIAL

Globe Artichokes with Garlic Butter

A classic and unfussy presentation, everything depends on the quality of the produce. When selecting artichokes, check the freshness of the cut on the stem and the leaves – they should be clean and waxy, not bruised, brown or dried out at the ends.

serves two

2 globe artichokes
1 lemon wedge
olive oil
100 g/4 oz unsalted butter
3 cloves of garlic, chopped

1. Cut the stems off the artichokes. Put in boiling water with a wedge of lemon and a drop of olive oil and boil for 25 minutes. Test for readiness by removing a leaf from near the base of the artichoke and nibbling to see if it is tender. If it is, drain the artichokes; if not, cook for another 5 minutes and test again.
2. Melt the butter. Add the chopped garlic and warm through, but do not really fry it.
3. Sit the artichokes upright on two plates, then pour the garlic butter over them so that it trickles down between the leaves.
4. Eat by removing the leaves one by one, sucking and scraping off the buttery flesh at the end of each leaf with your teeth (laborious but wonderful). When you get to the centre, cut away the hairy parts with a knife and eat the heart.

Carrot and Cumin Soup

serves four

50 g/2 oz butter
2 onions, peeled and finely chopped
1 clove of garlic, peeled and chopped
large pinch of saffron threads, crushed and soaked in 2 tbspn warm water
1 tspn ground cumin
pinch of cumin seeds
salt and freshly ground black pepper
900 g/2 lb carrots, peeled and diced
225 ml/8 fl oz white wine
1 litre/1 ¾ pints good chicken or vegetable stock
4 tspn thick Greek yoghurt
half a handful of fresh flat-leaf parsley leaves, chopped

1. Melt the butter in a large pan, add the onions and sweat for a few minutes until they start to soften.
2. Add the garlic, saffron, ground cumin, cumin seeds, salt and black pepper. Cook gently, stirring occasionally, for about 15 minutes until the onions are soft and golden, but don't let them burn.
3. Add the carrots and cook gently for a couple of minutes, then pour in the wine, bring to the boil and allow to bubble for a couple of minutes.
4. Add the stock and bring to the boil again. Turn down the heat and simmer until the carrots are soft (about 10 minutes).
5. Liquidize the soup in a blender and return to the heat until hot, but do not reboil. Check for seasoning.
6. Divide the soup between four bowls. Put a teaspoon of Greek yoghurt in each and sprinkle on a little flat-leaf parsley.

Sea Bass Baked with Fennel, Lemon and Thyme

This recipe, improvised entirely by Selina (and certainly open to further improvisation by you), is one of many in this book that I have since cooked several times at home. I like to eat it cold, with the same saffron and lemon mayonnaise, as an outdoorsy summer dish. Cold sea bass is far better than cold salmon.

serves two

4 tbspn olive oil

2 small sea bass, approximately 350–400g/ 12-14 oz each, gutted and scaled

2 bulbs of fennel, cut downwards into medium slices

bunch of fresh thyme

zest of one lemon

2 bay leaves

salt and freshly ground black pepper

1. Preheat the oven to 200°C/400°F/Gas mark 6.
2. Lightly rub a shallow baking dish with a little of the olive oil.
3. Stuff the fish with sliced fennel, a couple of sprigs of thyme, half the lemon zest and one bay leaf in each. Scatter more thyme and the rest of the lemon zest above and below the fish. Season the fish well, inside and out, with salt and pepper, and trickle over the olive oil.
4. Loosely cover the dish with foil and place in the oven. After 10 minutes, remove the foil to crisp the skin. The fish should be ready 10 minutes later.
5. Serve with saffron and lemon mayonnaise and warm potato and olive salad (recipes follow).

Saffron and Lemon Mayonnaise

A lovely golden mayonnaise.

serves 4

yolk of 1 large free-range egg

large pinch of saffron threads, crushed and soaked in 2 tbspn warm water

grated zest of 1 lemon

salt and pepper

150 ml / ¼ pt extra virgin olive oil (or half and half olive and sunflower oil)

1–3 tspn lemon juice

1. Put the egg yolk, soaked saffron threads, lemon zest, salt and pepper in a food processor and whiz up.
2. Keeping the motor going, drizzle in the oil very slowly. The mayonnaise will become thick and creamy.
3. Add lemon juice to taste and check the seasoning.
4. If not using a food processor, put the egg yolk, saffron, lemon zest, salt and pepper into a mixing bowl and use a hand or electric whisk to mix them together. Whisk in the oil, a drop at a time until about half the oil has been added and then in a slow, thin trickle for the rest of the oil.
5. Serve the mayonnaise with the sea bass or any other hot or cold fish.

Warm potato and olive salad ▲

Warm Potato and Olive Salad

serves two

450 g/1 lb small new potatoes, washed

4 shallots

3 tbspn olive oil

a dozen large black olives (ideally calamata), halved and destoned

salt and freshly ground black pepper

1. Put the potatoes in well-salted boiling water.
2. Meanwhile, slice the shallots and fry for a few minutes in the olive oil until softened and golden brown.
3. Drain the potatoes when they are still just this side of done and add to the frying pan with the black olives.
4. Fry the potatoes gently until they are slightly caramelized. Season with salt and black pepper.
5. Serve with the sea bass, or other fish, or just about anything else, in fact.

Leek, Goat's Cheese and Mustard Tart

Adapted from The Greens Cookbook, *by Deborah Madison.*

serves four

pastry case

225 g/8 oz plain flour (organic if possible)

100 g/4 oz chilled unsalted butter

1 free-range egg, beaten

filling

50 g/2 oz butter

450g/1 lb leeks washed thoroughly and cut into 6 mm /¼ in rings

120 ml/4 fl oz white wine or water

salt and freshly ground black pepper

2 free-range eggs

225 ml/8 fl oz double cream or crème fraîche

2 tbspn coarse-grained mustard

handful of chopped chives

100 g/4 oz goat's cheese

To make the pastry case

1. Blend the flour and butter together in a food processor until the mixture resembles fine breadcrumbs (or rub together by hand the old-fashioned way).
2. Add the egg to bind and mix everything together to form a ball. Wrap the pastry in foil or greaseproof paper and leave to rest in the fridge for at least half an hour.
3. Roll out the pastry on a floured surface. Put into a 23 cm/ 9 in baking tin and place in the fridge or freezer for 15 minutes.
4. Heat oven to 190°C/375°F/Gas mark 5.
5. Line the pastry with foil and cover with dried chickpeas, beans or purpose-made clay baking beans (this is known as baking blind). Place in the centre of the oven for 20 minutes. Remove foil and beans carefully and cook for another 2 minutes. You can make the pastry case in advance or prepare the tart filling while the pastry case is cooking.

To make the filling

6. Melt the butter in a large frying pan or wide saucepan. Add the leeks and sweat for two minutes.
7. Add the wine or water, a pinch of salt and a twist of black pepper. Cook until the leeks are tender (about 15 minutes), adding more liquid if needed to stop them drying out or burning. You want a creamy, slightly runny consistency.
8. Beat the eggs and mix well with the cream, mustard, leeks, half the chives and half the goat's cheese.
9. Pour the filling into the pastry shell and scatter the remaining chives and goat's cheese on top. Add more cheese if necessary to get a good mixture of yellow mustard-cream, green leeks and white cheese.
10. Cook for approximately 20-25 minutes at the same temperature in the oven until the top is firm and golden brown.
11. Serve hot, warm or cold with oven-roasted tomatoes (recipe follows).

Oven-roasted Tomatoes

Anyone who finds tomatoes too often insipid and lacking in flavour will discover that this process transforms them, concentrating the flavour beautifully.

serves four

12 tomatoes

salt and freshly ground black pepper

3 or 4 tbspn balsamic vinegar

3 or 4 tbspn extra virgin olive oil

1. Preheat the oven to 180°C/350°F/Gas mark 4.
2. Cut the tomatoes in half horizontally and put in a single layer on a baking tray, cut side up. Sprinkle with salt and pepper.
3. Sprinkle over balsamic vinegar and slosh over extra virgin olive oil. Place in the oven for 10-15 minutes, until the tomatoes are lightly browned and the juices are syrupy.
4. Serve with leek, goat's cheese and mustard tart, or just on toast with an extra trickle of olive oil.

Prune and Armagnac Tart

Idriss, at 16 Grande Rue, was perhaps Selina's favourite shop in Boulogne, selling nothing but dried fruit and nuts of supreme quality and dazzling appearance. The Agen prunes she bought were the plumpest, juiciest and most flavourful I have ever encountered, transforming this tart from something special into something sensational.

Vary the recipe with the season. Cherries soaked in Marsala are good in the summer, for example.

serves four–eight, depending on greed!

approximately 15 plump prunes (ideally from Agen)

120 ml/4 fl oz/a generous wine glass of Armagnac

pastry case

225 g/8 oz plain flour (preferably organic)

2 tbspn caster sugar

100 g/4 oz chilled unsalted butter

1 free-range egg

custard filling

200 ml/7 fl oz tub crème fraîche

80 g/3 oz caster sugar

3 free-range eggs

few drops of vanilla essence or use sugar that has had a vanilla pod stored in it

1 Soak the prunes in Armagnac for at least an hour, or overnight if they are very dry. Remove any stones.

To make the pastry case

2 Blend together the flour, sugar and butter in a food processor or by hand until the mixture resembles breadcrumbs.

3 With the motor running, add the egg to bind the mixture together. Chill the pastry for at least half an hour.

4 Roll out the pastry on a floured surface and line a 23 cm / 9 in bnaking tin. Put in the fridge or freezer for 15 minutes, then blind bake as for the savoury tart case on page 27.

To make the filling

5 Blend the crème fraîche, sugar, eggs and vanilla essence together in a food processor or by hand with a balloon whisk.

6 Drain the prunes and put in the bottom of the cooked pastry case, then pour over the custard mixture.

7 Bake for 30-40 minutes until firm and golden. Serve warm or at room termperature.

Chocolate and Hazelnut Biscotti

Adapted from One Year at Books for Cooks *by Jill Dupleix, illustrated by Selina Snow.*

makes about 20 biscuits

200 g/7 oz plain flour (organic if possible)
170 g/6 oz cocoa powder
3–4 tspn baking powder
pinch of salt
225 g/8 oz caster sugar
3–4 tbspn ground espresso coffee
grated rind of 1 orange
50 g/2 oz plain chocolate (with high cocoa content)
2 free-range eggs
3–4 tspn vanilla essence
100 g/4 oz hazelnuts

1. Preheat the oven to 180°C/350°F/Gas mark 4 and cover a baking sheet with parchment paper.
2. Put the flour, cocoa powder, baking powder, salt, sugar, coffee, orange rind and chocolate in a food processor. Process in short bursts (using the pulse option if you have it) until the mixture is a fine powder. If not using a food processor, mix the ingredients together by hand, finely chopping or grating the chocolate first.
3. With the motor running, slowly pour in the eggs and vanilla until the dough pulls together. If working by hand, mix the eggs and vanilla into the mixture with a wooden spoon.
4. Take the dough out of the processor and place on a lightly floured surface. Knead in the hazelnuts.
5. Roll out the dough into a log 45 cm/18 in long and approximately 10 cm/4 in in diameter. Dust lightly with flour all over and place on the baking sheet.
6. Bake for 25-30 minutes until firm. Take out of the oven, remove baking parchment and leave the biscuit log to cool.
7. Turn the oven down to 150°C/300°F/Gas mark 2.
8. Cut the log into slices approximately 2 cm/¾ in wide, at an angle. Place the biscuits in a single layer on a baking sheet and bake for a further 15 minutes, until dried out completely.
9. Serve with ice-cream (vanilla is especially good), or dunked into Vin Santo, Amaretto or small cups of strong black coffee.

Prune and Armagnac tart ▶

SOME LIKE IT HOT

Steve Donovan and Eddie Baines

MENU

Chunky guacamole
Habanero and pineapple salsa
Tortilla chips

Stuffed ancho chillies
Red chilli sauce
Chipotle and soured cream sauce

Grilled shark steaks marinated in lime
Mole sauce
Rice
Refried beans

Lime and chilli sorbet

How can I describe Steve and Eddie? I would say they are a couple of nuts, but then Eddie would probably interrupt me and say, 'No, we're not. We're a couple of chillies.' And then Steve would add, 'Or maybe a couple of chilli nuts.'

Steve and Eddie are something of a double act. They share the same passions – or obsessions, depending on whether you take their point of view or that of their wives. Either way, the topics of most of their slightly competitive banter, not to mention their marathon telephone conversations, are rock'n'roll, 1950s American cars, hair wax, original Lee Jeans, baseball and softball, beer, and – the big one – *chillies.*

Steve infuriates Eddie by always taking 'the chilli thing' one stage further than he expects. 'Eddie and I talked about making some chilli T-shirts,' Steve told me, 'for ourselves and maybe a few of our friends. And now I'm producing a whole range of T-shirts under the name of Chilli Obsessed.'

'Yeah,' added Eddie, giving Steve his characteristic suspicious sideways glance, 'which labels you quite well. And being a brewer,' he turned to me, 'I taught Steve how to make beer. And just to show how well he'd learned the brewer's art, he went and made a home-brew chilli stout, which I have to admit is pretty good.' To cap it all, Steve has started his own softball team, which he called the Langtoft Chillies.

But despite their long-standing mutual interest, the two of them had never actually cooked chillies together in the same kitchen until they came to make this special meal. And they were mightily excited about it! Chillies weren't just on the menu, they *were* the menu – from the appetizer of home-made tortilla chips with pineapple and chilli salsa, right down to the sweet with a sting: lime and chilli sorbet.

The problem was to keep reminding themselves who this dinner was really for – not the Steve and Eddie Chilli Appreciation Society, as much of the banter in the kitchen might have suggested, but their devoted and extremely tolerant wives, Sue and Gina.

Steve and Eddie got married on the same day, one year apart, ten and nine years ago respectively. This dinner was to be a double anniversary celebration.

Steve's wife, Sue, who was banished from her own kitchen during the preparation, was just a little sceptical about how much attention the girls were going to get come dinnertime. 'When the two of them get together,' she said, 'nobody else gets much of a look in. They forget you're there.'

'At least we should get something nice to eat,' said Eddie's wife, Gina, looking on the bright side. 'They're both good cooks.'

But Steve and Eddie had a few romantic aces up their sleeves, which Sue and Gina hadn't bargained for. For a start, they dusted down their wedding suits and squeezed into them (a tight squeeze in Eddie's case) for the first time in almost a decade. But the winning move, quite unexpected by their wives, was the hiring of a genuine mariachi band in full Colombian regalia that swept into the kitchen over the sorbet and launched into romantic seranades.

And I can tell you, the sight of the two couples, holding hands across the table while the mariachi band strummed and wailed, was enough to melt anybody's heart – as if the chillies hadn't already done that.

A Note on Chillies

The imported dried chillies required for these and other Mexican recipes are specialist ingredients which may take some finding. However, as Mexican food increases in popularity, they are slowly becoming more widely available. You may find them in upmarket delis and specialist food stores, and even in the larger supermarkets, especially in London. But a regular supply of the best quality chillies is always available by mail order from The Cool Chile Company, PO Box 5702, London W10 6WE (tel: 0973 311714).

While handling raw chillies, be careful not to touch any sensitive part of your body, from your eyes downwards, and wash your hands thoroughly afterwards. People with broken skin or cuts on their fingers should handle raw chillies with gloves.

Chunky Guacamole

Steve and Eddie like to keep their guacamole and salsas chunky rather than smooth and to use lots of aromatic fresh coriander. Avocados for guacamole should be soft and ripe, but cut out any black bits.

serves four

½ large red onion, finely chopped
5 spring onions, chopped
1 clove of garlic, minced
2 large ripe avocados, peeled and chopped
5 ripe tomatoes, peeled, deseeded and chopped
juice of 2 limes
generous handful fresh coriander (mostly leaves), roughly chopped

1. Put all the ingredients together in a bowl and mix well with a wooden spoon. The more you mix, the more puréed the avocado becomes. Stop when it gets how you like it.
2. Serve with soured cream, tortilla chips (recipe follows) and habanero and pineapple salsa (recipe follows).

◀ Tortilla chips with habanero and pineapple salsa

Habanero and Pineapple Salsa

Habaneros are the head honchos of hot chillies. This salsa mitigates the heat but does not kill the kick. A habanero heat sits on the front of the tongue in a long afterburn. A glass of milk or a dollop of soured cream will cool things down far better than water or beer, though Steve and Eddie persist optimistically with the beer option!

serves four

- *1 red onion, finely chopped*
- *2 tomatoes, roughly chopped*
- *½ –1 fresh fresh habanero (or Scotch bonnet) chilli, deseeded and finely chopped*
- *1 ripe fresh pineapple, peeled, cored and cut into 12 mm /½ in cubes*
- *1 red pepper, roughly chopped*
- *1 yellow pepper, roughly chopped*
- *juice of 2–3 limes or ½ grapefruit*
- *2 cloves of garlic, finely chopped*
- *1 tspn salt*
- *2 generous handfuls of fresh coriander leaves, coarsely chopped*

1. Mix all the ingredients except the coriander. Let all the flavours mingle for an hour.
2. Add the coriander, freshly chopped, at the last moment, and mix again before serving.
3. Serve with tortilla chips (recipe follows), guacamole (recipe above) and soured cream.

Tortillas

You really do need to use fresh masa harina flour, available by mail order or in speciality shops, to get the robustly earthy flavour of real tortililas.

makes 8

- *225 g/8 oz masa harina (Mexican corn flour)*
- *approximately 350 ml/ 12 fl oz water*

1. Mix the flour and water together by hand, using enough water to get a dough which is soft, pliable and slightly moist.
2. Rest for at least 10 minutes to make sure all the water has been absorbed by the flour.
3. Divide into eight balls. Make into discs using a tortilla press, or use Eddie's improvised alternative. Put a plastic place mat on the work surface and a plastic sandwich bag on top. Put a ball of dough on the sandwich bag and cover with another one. Press down on the tortilla dough ball with another place mat to make a thin, flat disc, about 2–3 mm/⅛ in thick. Peel the plastic off the tortilla.
4. Cook the tortillas on a hot, dry skillet for 30 seconds each side or until brown spots appear on the dough. If the mixture bubbles up while cooking, press it down with a fish slice or the back of a spoon.
5. Serve while still warm as a scoop or accompaniment to all Mexican food.

Tortilla Chips

Fresh tortilla chips, much tastier and subtler than the processed ones, are easy to make once you get into the swing of it.

makes 64

8 slightly stale tortillas

frying oil, e.g. sunflower oil

2 tspn rock salt

a tiny pinch of cinnamon (optional)

1. Leave the tortillas out overnight to make them slightly stale. Cut each into quarters, then each quarter into half, to get eight triangles.
2. Heat a couple of inches of oil to 160–180°C. Put one chip in to test. It should start sizzling immediately but without burning. Fry the tortilla pieces until crisp, turning once (about 45-60 seconds in all).
3. Shake the tortillas in a bag with the rock salt and, if you like, a tiny pinch of cinnamon.
4. Serve with soured cream, guacamole (recipe above) and salsa (recipe above).

Stuffed Ancho Chillies

Some people are intimidated by chillies. Eddie swears these stuffed anchos, with their fruity piquancy, are the recipe to win over any doubters. And Sue and Gina adored them!

serves four as a starter

- *4 ancho chillies*
- *8 tbspn refried beans (recipe follows)*
- *6 chopped spring onions*
- *2 tbspn minced sun-dried tomatoes*
- *50 g/2 oz mature Cheddar cheese, coarsely grated*
- *2 tbspn lime juice*
- *3 cloves of garlic, minced*
- *½ tspn ground black pepper*

1 Preheat the oven to 200°C/400°F/Gas mark 6.

Note: Since these chillies are to be stuffed, the preparation procedure is a slight variation on that described on p.40.

2 Soak the ancho chillies in hot water for about 15 minutes or until pliable. Do not over-soak because the chillies need to be a firm casing for the stuffing. Drain and carefully make a slit down one side of each chilli. Deseed and devein, but keep the stalks on. Roast the chillies for a few minutes in a hot pan. Soak in warm water a second time for about 5 minutes (this makes them more pliable for stuffing), then drain and dry.

3 Mix together the refried beans, spring onions, sun-dried tomatoes, cheese, lime juice, garlic and pepper. Divide the mixture into four equal parts and stuff carefully into the chillies. Wrap some tin foil around the stalk ends to stop them burning and lay the chilllies in a baking dish.

4 Cook in the oven for about 15-20 minutes until the chillies are browned but not burnt. Remove the foil from the stalk end before serving.

5 Serve with red chilli sauce and a dollop of soured cream mixed with chipotle sauce (recipes follow).

Red Chilli Sauce

A dark-red sauce which looks good next to a dollop of pink chipotle soured cream.

makes more than enough to accompany the stuffed chillies above. Any surplus can be refrigerated and kept for up to 2 weeks

- *3 dried guajillo chilles*
- *4 tomatoes*
- *3 large cloves of garlic*
- *½ tspn cumin seeds*
- *2 tspn fresh oregano leaves*
- *salt*

1 Toast, deseed, devein and soak the chillies in the usual way (see p.40). Drain, reserving the soaking water.

2 Cut the tomatoes in half and place on a lightly oiled skillet, or under a hot grill, until nicely blackened, for a barbecue-charred taste. Similarly blacken the whole garlic cloves.

3 Dry roast the cumin seeds in a heavy frying pan or skillet for a few minutes over a high heat, then grind to a powder with a pestle and mortar.

4 Blend the chillies, tomatoes and garlic in a blender with the oregano, a pinch of salt and between 150 and 290 ml/¼ and ½ pint of the chilli soaking water.

5 Put the sauce in hot pan and fry, stirring with a wooden spoon or spatula to avoid sticking, until it is reduced down to a thick pouring consistency.

Grilled shark steaks marinated in lime with mole sauce ▶

Chipotle Sauce

Chipotles are jalapeño peppers that have been dried by smoking, giving them an incredibly powerful, smoky-tobacco flavour. They are Steve's favourite chillies, and he regularly makes a batch of this intense, smoky hot sauce and keeps it in ice-cube trays in the freezer. A cube or two adds flavour to sauces, salsas and other dishes. The sauce can be 'diluted' with soured cream and this is what Steve serves with his stuffed ancho-chillies. I like it with sausages and even cheese on toast.

enough for 2 ice-cube trays

- *8 chipotle chillies*
- *1 onion, finely chopped*
- *5 cloves of garlic*
- *5 tbspn cider/malt vinegar*
- *1 tbspn tomato purée*
- *¼ tspn salt*
- *290–425ml /½–¾ pint water*
- *150 ml/¼ pt soured cream (optional)*

1. Toast, deseed, devein and soak the chillies in the usual way (see below). Drain.
2. Put in a saucepan with the onion, garlic, vinegar, tomato purée, salt and water. Simmer uncovered for an hour.
3. Whiz up the paste in a blender to get a purée. Return to a pan and cook for a few minutes to get a thick pouring consistency. Store in ice-cube trays in the freezer.
4. To make chipotle cream, defrost one cube of frozen sauce and strain away any excess liquid. Mix with 150 ml/¼ pint of soured cream.

Mole Sauce

Mexican mole sauces are all about the art of blending. A large number of powerfully flavoured ingredients are combined in such a way that all contribute but none predominates. In Mexico, mole is served on all special occasions. Steve and Eddie have adapted the classic mole for non-meat eaters, substituting chicken stock with Steve's home-made chilli beer (stout will do) and serving it with shark marinated in lime. This sauce can be made well in advance. It will keep for up to two weeks in the fridge and if anything improves over time.

***Note**: The following procedure is the standard preparation for most dried chillies prior to cooking.*

serves four

- *2 dried passilla chillies*
- *2 dried mulato chillies*
- *2 ancho chillies*
- *5 tbspn sesame seeds*

1. On a dry cast-iron skillet (or heavy frying pan), toast the chillies over a high heat for a few minutes, turning occasionally. Split open the chillies, remove the seeds and stalk and, using your fingernails or a small knife, pare off the thicker veins. Rinse well. Put the chillies into a bowl and pour over just enough boiling water to cover. Leave to soak for 30 minutes to an hour. Drain, reserving the soaking liquid.
2. Dry roast the sesame seeds over a medium heat in a skillet or heavy frying pan until they begin to pop, stirring quickly. Remove from the pan. Put aside 2 tbspn of the

¼ tspn whole coriander seeds

1 star anise

3 cm/1 in cinnamon stick

3 whole cloves

1 tspn sunflower oil

50 g/2 oz whole almonds with skins

80 g/3 oz raisins

salt

1 tbspn tomato paste

1 small onion, finely chopped

45 g/1½ oz Mexican chocolate (or highest-grade dark chocolate)

290 ml/½ pint chilli ale 'Smoky Dog' (or good dark stout)

seeds for decorating the end dish.

3 Dry roast the coriander seeds, star anise, cinnamon stick and cloves for a short while until they start to change colour and become fragrant (around 30 seconds). Remove from the pan.
4 Put a little sunflower oil into the skillet and toast the almonds for a few minutes, taking care not to burn them. Dry on some paper. Add the raisins to the pan and cook until they puff up. Dry on kitchen paper.
5 Grind together all the spices in a coffee grinder or pound with a pestle and mortar.
6 Put the ground spices in a blender and add the chillies, about half of the liquid in which they have been soaking, a large pinch of salt, the almonds, sultanas, tomato paste and chopped onion. Whiz up in the blender to get a smooth paste.
7 Put the paste in a hot skillet and fry gently. Add the chocolate and the chilli beer or stout.
8 Simmer the sauce slowly for about 45 minutes, stirring occasionally to prevent it sticking to the pan. If the sauce becomes too thick, add a little more beer or more of the chilli soaking water. You want to get a thick pouring consistency which slides off the spoon.
9 Put some sauce on each plate and scatter on the reserved sesame seeds. Serve with shark marinated in lime (recipe follows). It is equally delicious with other simply grilled fish – particularly fresh swordfish or tuna – or with chicken or turkey.

Grilled Shark Steaks Marinated in Lime

Shark is a strong, meaty fish which stands up well to the flavour of the sauce.

serves four

2 x 400–500 g/14–16 oz shark steaks

2 limes

salt and freshly ground black pepper

1 Remove the skin and central cartilage from the shark steaks and cut each in half to get four portions.
2 Grate the zest from the two limes sparingly – try to avoid scraping into the white pith, which is bitter. Squeeze the limes. Reserve a pinch of the zest and 1 tspn of the juice.
3 Marinate the fish in the rest of the lime juice and zest for not more than one hour (otherwise the fish will become too soft).
4 Heat a cast-iron grill pan (the kind with raised ridges is ideal) or heavy frying pan pan until it is very hot. Wipe excess marinade off the steaks and place them on the pan (unless you have a very large pan, you will probably be able to cook only two at a time). Cook for about 3 minutes on each side. Season with salt and pepper before and after turning.
5 Just before serving, dress each shark steak with a little extra lime juice and a pinch of zest. Serve with the mole sauce and a crisp green salad.

Refried Beans

serves six

170 g/6 oz black kidney beans or pinto beans

1–2 tbspn vegetable oil

80 g/3 oz mature Cheddar (or manchego), grated

salt and freshly ground black pepper

1 Soak the dried beans in plenty of cold water overnight. Change the water and bring to the boil, cooking at a full rolling boil for at least 45 minutes or until tender (with dried beans that have been hanging around for a long time this can take up to 2 hours). It does not matter if the beans are over-cooked because they are going to be mashed up. Drain.

2 Put the cooked beans in 1 tbspn oil and cook over a medium heat, mashing every so often with a potato masher so they absorb the oil. Add a little more oil if the beans get too dry. Continue until you get a dryish, thick, heavy bean paste.

3 Mash in the cheese and season with salt and pepper. Cook for another minute, mixing thoroughly, and check seasoning.

4 Refried beans are used in all kinds of Mexican dishes, but a satisfyingly simple way to serve them is to fill a taco shell or soft tortilla, add extra cheese, melt in a hot oven for a few minutes and serve with red chilli sauce (recipe above) at one end, soured cream at the other, and lots of guacamole (recipe above) in the middle.

Lime and Chilli Sorbet

A sorbet which sounds hot but tastes refreshingly cool.

serves four

350 g/12 oz caster sugar

200 ml/6 fl oz water

zest of four limes

200 ml/6 fl oz lime juice (approximately 12 limes)

1 fresh, mild green chilli

1 fresh, mild red chilli

1 egg white

1 Add the sugar to the water and stir over a low heat until it has dissolved. Bring to the boil and bubble rapidly for 5 minutes to make a light syrup. Throw in the lime zest and leave to cool.

2 Meanwhile, deseed the chillies and chop into very thin strips, about 1 cm/½ in long. Blanch in boiling water to remove the heat. Put in cold water. The heat should be almost gone; the chillies are more for colour and texture.

3 Stir the lime juice into the syrup. At this point you can add the chilli pieces and the egg white and pour the mixture into an ice-cream machine until frozen. Alternatively use the traditional 'freeze and whisk' method. Do not add the chillies and egg white yet, but transfer the mixture into a mixing bowl and put in the freezer for about an hour or until partially frozen. Remove from the freezer, and whisk the frozen bits back into the syrup. Replace in the freezer allow to part-freeze once more, then remove and whisk again. Now the mixture should be thick and slushy.

4 Whisk the egg white to form soft peaks. Carefully fold into the part frozen sorbet, then fold in the chilli pieces. Return to the freezer and leave until completely frozen. Remove from freezer 30 minutes before serving to soften.

◀ Chillies and baseball are Steve and Eddie's principal obsessions

CARIBBEAN BIRTHDAY SURPRISE

Tricia Wallace and Alison Haughton

MENU

Guinness punch
Saltfish fritters
Saltfish and ackee vol-au-vents

Jerk pork
Rice and peas
Fried plantains
Salad

Pat's coconut pie
Tropical fruit salad

Food, as everyone knows, is a great bonding agent for friendship. But while sharing food with friends is a fundamental pleasure of civilized society, cooking with them in a shared kitchen space is not always such a breeze. Someone usually wants to be boss — and that's where the trouble starts.

So watching Tricia and Alison cooking together in happiness and harmony was a revelation. What made it particularly satisfying was that all this care and attention in the kitchen was by way of a birthday surprise for their friend Amaka (Tricia's flatmate), who suspected absolutely nothing. (We almost got rumbled when I went to meet the girls with our researcher at Tricia's house a few days before the shoot. Amaka turned up unexpectedly, but such is university life that she wasn't the least bit curious about what two complete strangers were doing in her flat.)

Tricia and Alison are both second-year students at Birmingham University. Tricia was 'fairly fed up' for most of the first year — a familiar story of living in university accommodation with students you don't know. 'Each person had their own food shelf in the cupboard and in the fridge,' she told me, 'and no one was interested in sharing anything. It was like living alongside people, not with them.'

At the beginning of the second year, Tricia moved into a five- bedroom house in the leafy suburb of Bearwood with four girlfriends she had made through the African and Caribbean Society: 'Straightaway I became "Mum". That's what they call me, because I'm always cooking these huge meals. People come in, not just my flatmates — all sorts of people seem to end up here — and they'll say, "What's cooking, Mum?" '

Alison was an early visitor, and found herself hanging out in the kitchen with Tricia for hours on end. 'Now it's got to the stage where, if we're not actually cooking together, I'll ring Tricia up to ask her if she's making anything, or to arrange to go food shopping the next day.' Both girls have mobile phones, which means they can get on line and talk turkey whenever the mood takes them.

Tricia and Alison are now rediscovering their own food culture and go regularly to the city market to find the best possible ingredients for traditional Caribbean cooking. 'I guess we're still learning to shop,' Tricia explained, 'how to tell when things are ripe, and ready, and good. It's an adventure in itself.'

They are very natural cooks, putting together their ingredients with a lot of enthusiasm and a minimum of fuss. Their guests knew to expect something special and kept trying to barge into the kitchen to get a sneak preview. The saltfish and ackee vol-au-vents were consumed as fast as I could fill the little cases, and most had been devoured by the time the Birthday Girl arrived.

The surprise went like clockwork. Amaka thought her boyfriend, Chris, was taking her out to dinner, *à deux*. As they approached the party, he got her to put a blindfold on, led her out of the car and steered her into the garden. When her blindfold was removed, Amaka seemed entirely unfazed by the camera that was pointing at her. The surprise and excitement were reserved for her friends. 'I thought they'd all forgotten me on my birthday,' she told me later. 'I should have realized that Tricia and Alison would be up to something. They're just the *best*.'

Saltfish Fritters

These spicy fritters are best served straight from the fryer, still hot and crisp. They are excellent with drinks, or a make a nice first course with a few lightly dressed green leaves to accompany. Saltfish (dried and salted white fish, usually cod) is not appetizing in its raw form: the rigid blocks have the texture of cardboard and smell like a wet dog. But soaked and reconstituted, it is transformed. The preparation does take a while but the wonderful savoury flavour of the end product is well worth the effort.

serves twelve as a canapé, eight as a starter

400 g/14 oz unsoaked saltfish

1 tbspn Caribbean fish seasoning (or substitute Worcestershire sauce)

1 tbspn soy sauce

225 g/8 oz self-raising flour

water

1 onion, finely diced

2 cloves of garlic, minced

2 spring onions, finely sliced

3 hot red chilli peppers, seeded and finely diced

2 tspn West Indian hot pepper sauce

1 tbspn all-purpose Jamaican seasoning

1–2 tbspn curry powder

vegetable oil for deep-frying

1. Soak the fish overnight. Drain, transfer to a pan with fresh water and bring to the boil. Drain. Add more fresh cold water and bring to the boil again. Repeat two or three times, tasting each time for saltiness. Leave to cool.
2. Separate the fish from the skin and bones and pull it into small pieces.
3. Season the fish with fish seasoning and soy sauce. Marinate for at least 20 minutes.
4. Sieve the flour into a mixing bowl and add enough water to make a thick, porridge-like batter. Beat hard with a wire whisk to get rid of any lumps.
5. Add the onion, garlic, spring onion, chilli pepper, hot pepper sauce, all-purpose seasoning and curry powder. Mix thoroughly.
6. Heat a few inches of vegetable oil in a deep pan so it is hot enough for deep-frying. Test by putting a little of the mixture into the pan. It should sizzle but not burn.
7. Spoon four or five mini-fritters into the pan at a time and cook until crisp and brown, turning once. Dry on kitchen paper and serve hot – but not burning hot!

Saltfish and ackee vol-au-vents ▶

Saltfish and Ackee Vol-au-vents

The yellow, red and green of this dish make it a colourful as well as an elegant canapé or starter. Ackee look a bit like scrambled eggs (they are also known as 'vegetable brains') and have a creamy texture. I'd never had them before, but was very taken with them. They are certainly worth seeking out in West Indian shops and ethnic grocers.

serves twelve as a canapé (two each) or six as starter (four each)

1 medium onion

5 tbspn cooked saltfish (see previous recipe for preparation)

½ red pepper, seeded and cut into 4 cm/1½ in long, thin slices

½ green pepper, seeded and cut into 4 cm/1½ in long, thin slices

2 fresh tomatoes, finely chopped

1 x 200 g/7 oz tin chopped tomatoes

170 g/6 oz tinned ackee

24 small vol-au-vent cases

green part of 2 spring onions, finely chopped

1. Fry the onion until soft.
2. Add the saltfish, red and green peppers (keeping a few back for decoration), fresh and tinned tomatoes and cook until reduced to a thick sauce.
3. Drain the ackee of any water from the tin, then stir into the tomato and pepper mixture until it is warmed through. Do not stir too vigorously as you don't want the ackee to break up.
4. Cook the vol-au-vent cases according to the packet instructions.
5. Reheat the sauce and fill the vol-au-vents. Garnish with chopped spring onions and slivers of red and green pepper.
6. Serve hot or warm.

Jerk Pork

One theory about the origins of the name for jerk pork is that the spicy flavours 'jerk' your taste buds. Another is that the meat, originally cooked in pits in the fields, was cooked dry so you jerked away bits of the dried pork in your mouth.

serves eight

2 tbspn soy sauce
1 scant tbspn sesame oil
4 tbspn vegetable oil
3 tspn jerk seasoning
1 tspn finely grated nutmeg
small bunch of thyme
8 lean pork steaks
6 spring onions, shredded
1 apple, quartered, peeled, cored and sliced
2 tbspn golden granulated sugar

To finish the sauce

150 ml/¼ pint water
2 tbspn tomato purée
½ tbspn cornflour (optional)
1 apple, peeled, cored and sliced
butter

1. Mix together the soy sauce, sesame oil, vegetable oil, jerk seasoning, nutmeg and thyme in a bowl to make a marinade. Add the pork, spring onions and apple and turn to coat well. Put in a baking dish and sprinkle the sugar on top.
2. Leave refrigerated to marinate for a few hours or overnight.
3. Preheat the oven to 200°C/400°F/Gas mark 6 or prepare a barbecue.
4. Pour/scrape off the marinade and reserve.
5. Either barbecue the meat for approximately 10 minutes on each side, until cooked, or roast it in the preheated oven for approximately 45 minutes–1 hour, covered, until cooked. Drain off the stock and brown the meat on a slightly higher temperature for 10 minutes.
6. To make the sauce, heat the marinade with the water and tomato purée. The sauce should be a rich red-brown colour. Boil to reduce it to a good thickness or thicken it with a little cornflour if desired.
7. Sauté the extra apple pieces in a little butter and add to the sauce at the last moment.
8. Serve the meat with sauce, rice and peas, fried plantains (recipes follow) and salad.

Jerk pork ▲

Rice and Peas

There are many variations on rice and peas in Caribbean cookery. This Jamaican version uses kidney beans instead of peas, which gives the dish a purply-pink colour and is particularly delicious with its flavourings of coconut and thyme.

serves six as a side dish

225 g/8 oz dried kidney beans

340 g/12 oz long-grain rice (American or basmati)

1 onion, finely chopped

1 Soak the kidney beans in water overnight.
2 Change the water. Bring to the boil and boil hard for 30 minutes to destroy toxins in the beans.
3 Turn down the heat until the beans are simmering and continue cooking until they are almost done. Drain, reserving the water.
4 Rinse the rice well. Put the rice, kidney beans and onion in a pan. Add the water in

75 g/3 oz coconut cream block, grated and dissolved in hot water

a few sprigs of fresh thyme or ½ tspn dried thyme

which the beans were cooked, topping it up if necessary, to get twice as much water by volume as rice and beans. Cook for about 10 minutes.

5. Add the coconut milk and thyme. Cook for another 10 minutes, or until all the liquid has been absorbed and the rice has cooked.
6. Serve on a big plate, surrounded by fried plantain slices (recipe follows).

Fried Plantains

Plantains are a large, starchy member of the banana family. When buying a plantain, make sure that the skin is black and it is tender when gently pressed (an unripe plantain can have a black skin), but not too soft or bruised by squeezing. If not quite ready to eat, plantains can be left to ripen on a window-sill.

serves eight

2–3 plantains

salt

1 tspn caster sugar

sunflower or other vegetable oil for frying

1. Peel and slice the plantain in 6 mm/¼ in thick slices, cut crossways at an angle. Sprinkle a little salt and sugar over each piece.
2. Heat 5 cm/2 in oil in a deep pan so it is hot enough for deep-frying (i.e. a little piece of bread will sizzle and start to brown after about 20 seconds).
3. Fry the plantain slices in batches for 2 or 3 minutes, turning over once, until browned.
4. Drain on kitchen paper, and sprinkle with more salt if wanted.

Pat's Coconut Pie

A recipe from Alison's mother, Pat, which was served as one of the birthday cakes at Amaka's surprise birthday dinner.

Pastry

225 g/8 oz plain flour

1 tbspn caster sugar

1 tbspn ground almonds

100 g/4 oz butter

a little cold water

Filling

290 ml/½ pint hot milk, or ½ milk and ½ double cream for a slightly richer pie

50 g/2 oz caster sugar

pinch of salt

pinch of ground nutmeg

100 g/4 oz fresh coconut flesh, grated

1 tspn vanilla essence

3 egg yolks, beaten

Topping

3 egg whites

100 g/4 oz caster sugar

½ tspn vanilla essence

pinch of cream of tartar

10 glacé cherries to decorate

1. Preheat the oven to 200°C/400°F/Gas mark 6.
2. Sift the flour into a bowl. Mix with the sugar and ground almonds.
3. Cut the butter into small pieces. Mix with the flour to get a breadcrumb texture. Add a little cold water and mix together to form a ball. Rest in the fridge for15 minutes.
4. Roll out the pastry and put into a 23 cm/9 in pastry case. Trim the edges, prick the base and refrigerate.
5. *Optional*: if you want the pastry crispy, you can bake the pastry case blind. Line with foil and pour in dried beans or clay baking beads. Bake for 15 minutes at 180°C/350°F/Gas mark 4. Remove the foil and beans, and return to the oven for 2 more minutes to dry out the pastry case. Remove and either add the filling straight away or set the pastry case aside until you are ready for it. (Then turn up the oven to 200°C/400°F/Gas mark 6 again for the tart.)
6. Mix together the hot milk, caster sugar, salt, nutmeg, coconut and vanilla essence. Slowly add the egg yolks, mixing well.
7. Pour into the pastry case (blind or otherwise) and bake in the oven for 10 minutes.
8. Reduce the oven heat to 170°C/325°F/Gas mark 3 and continue baking the pie for a further 35 minutes, or until the filling has set. Remove from oven and allow to cool.
9. Turn the oven back up to 200°C/400°F/Gas mark 6.
10. Whisk the egg whites until they hold peaks.
11. Slowly add the caster sugar, vanilla essence and cream of tartar, whisking as you go. Continue to beat until stiff.
12. Spread the meringue over the top of the filling, right to the edges.
13. Decorate with glacé cherries. Bake for 10 minutes, or until the top is bronzed.
14. Serve hot or cold.

Tropical Fruit Salad

A glamorous tropical fruit salad which is served in a hollowed-out pineapple.

serves six

1 pineapple

2 medium-sized ripe (but not squishy) mangoes, peeled and diced

2 bananas, thinly sliced

2 kiwi fruits, peeled and diced

1 ogen melon, peeled and cut into small cubes

2 capfuls of rum

caster sugar, to taste

zest and segments of 2 limes

1 tbspn honey, warmed to make it runny

1 bulb stem ginger in syrup, finely chopped, plus 1 tbspn of the gingery syrup

1. Cut the top off the pineapple. Carefully cut out the flesh and cut it into small pieces, discarding the tough central core.
2. Mix all the ingredients together. Chill for at least 30 minutes to let the flavours mingle.
3. Put as much fruit salad as possible in the pineapple.
4. Put the pineapple on a serving dish, surrounded by any fruit which did not fit in (usually quite a lot). Put the top back on the pineapple and serve.

Guinness Punch

A celebration drink. The sweetness and thickness of this drink are mitigated by the stout and lots of ice-cubes.

serves eight

1–2 cans of Guinness
420 ml/15 fl oz can vanilla-flavoured Nutriment drink
400 ml/14 fl oz can condensed milk
400 ml/14 fl oz can evaporated milk
½ nutmeg, finely grated
4 capfuls of rum
1 tspn vanilla essence
ice, to serve

1. Pour 1½ cans of Guinness into a mixing bowl.
2. Add the Nutriment drink, condensed milk, evaporated milk, nutmeg, rum and vanilla essence. Taste and add more Guinness if it is too sweet. Chill in the fridge for at least 2 hours.
3. Serve chilled with ice-cubes in long glasses.

Non-alcoholic Ginger Beer

A hot but non-alcoholic ginger beer which is really refreshing served with ice.

450 g/1 lb fresh root ginger
3 litres/5½ pints water
500 g/1 lb 2 oz caster sugar
juice of 3 lemons

1. Peel the ginger. Coarsely chop or grate, or chop up in a food processor.
2. Put the ginger in a big pan and add the water. Boil for 20 minutes.
3. Take off the heat, add the sugar to the mixture and stir until it has dissolved. Cool the liquid to room temperature.
4. Strain the liquid through a sieve lined with muslin or a clean J-cloth. Add the lemon juice.
5. Store in the fridge until the sediment settles.
6. Ladle off the clear ginger beer from the sediment. Bottle and keep in the fridge.
7. Serve chilled with ice and an extra slice of lemon. If you want it alcoholic, add a measure (or two) of Jamaican rum.

Pat's coconut pie ▶

SUNDAY BEST

Stewart Ibbotson

MENU

Yorkshire pudding with sage and shallots
Sweet onion gravy

Roast beef
Italian-style roast potatoes
Cauliflower cheese
Sage and onion bread pudding
Peas
Carrots

Cheeseboard, including Parmesan and pears

The cooking bug strikes in strange places and at strange times. As a sailor in the Royal Navy, Stewart could hardly boil an egg. But since the ship's cook worked only Monday to Friday, and since the captain and officers always insisted on a proper British Sunday roast lunch, it fell to the men of the duty watch to prepare it for them.

'So one weekend,' Stewart told me, as we propped up his very own bar in his Knaresborough house, 'it was my turn. And I really knew nothing about it. But I guess I must have remembered a bit about what my mother used to do, and how she used to use the juices from the meat to make the gravy for the Yorkshire pudding because I made a pretty good go of it. And the captain thought it was all right. He must have done, because I seemed to end up doing a lot of weekends, not just beef, but lamb and pork and sometimes we used to get a capon, like a big chicken, but you can't get them any more.'

Now Stewart works as a fireman, a profession where he gets to exercise his endless curiousity about food in surprising ways. 'When we get to a kitchen fire,' he admits, 'I have to resist the temptation to look in people's fridges. Or if the fire started in the oven, I can't help wondering what it was they burned.' He's spread his culinary sails a lot since the navy days, cooking 'all kinds of pasta, a fair few curries' and recently 'dabbling with spicy Thai things'.

But for all the modern influences, Stewart remains a devotee of the art of the Sunday roast and he has the routine down to T. It begins with a stroll up the hill, with his wife Judith and the dogs, to take in what Stewart believes is the finest view in Yorkshire (and therefore probably the world) – Knaresborough Gorge. Then it's home via the pub for a quick pint to set them up for the kitchen tasks ahead. And when the pudding batter is made and the veg have been prepped, the meat goes in and it's back to the pub, 'for the long wait'. Not too long, of course, because the potatoes have to go in, and anyway Stewart likes his beef nice and pink in the middle.

Like all good cooks, Stewart cares passionately about the quality of his ingredients – and none more so than the meat itself. 'I like my beef properly matured – that means hung for at least three weeks. And that can be hard to get unless you have a good relationship with your butcher.' Fortunately, the butcher is a friend. 'He even comes to lunch sometimes,' says Stewart, 'to eat his own beef. And he likes my Yorkshire pudding – although the sage and shallots were a bit of a surprise for him.' Stewart may be a traditionalist, but he's not hidebound.

So once you've got the joint, I wondered, what's the magic formula for perfect roast beef? 'Salt,' said Stewart. 'Just a sprinkling on each side of the meat. I don't brown it – the oven's hot enough to do that – and I don't add any herbs or garlic. It's the flavour of the meat we're after. So just salt, and in it goes.' It's that simple? 'Definitely. When you've got something this good,' says Stewart, 'you really don't need to do much to it.'

And that's about as good a rule for successful cooking as I could put in one sentence.

Yorkshire Pudding with Sage and Shallots

Yorkshire pudding is traditionally eaten in Yorkshire as a starter before the roast, served with gravy. The idea originally was to take the edge off the appetite, especially children's, so that nobody would be too hungry for the expensive meat that followed. Stewart has departed from tradition by adding sage and shallots to the batter, an idea picked up from his mother-in-law.

serves six–eight as a starter

225 g/8 oz plain flour

4 medium eggs

290 ml/½ pint milk

290 ml/½ pint water

4 small shallots, finely chopped

1½ tbspn finely chopped fresh sage or 1 tbspn dried sage

1½ tspn salt

freshly ground black pepper

75 g/3 oz lard, beef dripping or sunflower oil

1. Sift the flour into a large mixing basin and make a well in the middle. Add the eggs, one at time, beating them into the flour with a fork. Bring in the flour gradually from the sides of the bowl and you should be able to avoid lumpiness.
2. Whisking constantly, slowly add enough milk and water to make a smooth batter the consistency of double cream.
3. Add the shallots and sage. Season with salt and pepper.
4. Leave covered with a tea-towel for at least 30 minutes and preferably for 1½ hours.
5. Preheat the oven to 230°C/450°F/Gas mark 8.
6. Put a large knob of lard or beef dripping in 2 x 20 cm/8 in round metal tins. Put in the oven until the fat starts to smoke (usually at least 15 minutes).
7. Pour the batter into the tins so that it covers the bottom but is no more than 1 cm/ ½ in deep. You can reserve the rest of the batter to thicken the sweet onion gravy (recipe follows).
8. Cook in the oven for 10–12 minutes, or until the puddings are puffed up, brown and crisp, turning round halfway through cooking.
9. Serve with sweet onion gravy.

◀ Yorkshire pudding with sage and shallots

Sweet Onion Gravy

This recipe was inspired by the chef Gary Rhodes, who is one of Stewart's culinary heroes for championing traditional British food. The onions are cooked gently for a very long time so they caramelize to a delicious savoury sweetness. Stewart says it is well worth the wait.

serves six

2 tbspn sunflower oil, lard or dripping
4 large onions, finely sliced
150 ml/5 fl oz water
850 ml/1½ pints beef stock (recipe follows)
thickener if required (1–2 tbspn of the Yorkshire pudding batter or cornflour)
juices from the joint
a knob/15 g/½ oz butter

1. Melt the fat in large saucepan or heavy frying pan over a medium heat and add the onions. Fry gently, stirring frequently to prevent sticking, until they are soft and well reduced in volume. Add a little water and go on cooking, stirring occasionally. The onions will slowly caramelize and turn sweet and golden. Whenever they seem in danger of getting too dry, or burning, add a little more of the water. You can go on cooking for up 2 hours, to get the softness, sweetness and caramel taste you want.
2. Add the stock. Turn up the heat and bubble to reduce for anything up to 30 minutes, until you have a sweet, beefy, oniony gravy. Thicken if you like by stirring in the Yorkshire pudding batter or a little cornflour.
3. Add the meat juices from the roasting joint and a knob of butter to glaze.
4. Serve half with the Yorkshire pudding and save the rest to serve with the roast beef.

Roast Beef

Choosing Beef

Whatever cut of beef you like, it will be both more tender and more tasty if it has been properly matured by hanging. Good butchers understand this and should be able to help you, especially if you shop with them regularly. Talk to them so they understand your needs. Some supermarkets now sell beef, usually labelled 'traditional', that has been more fully matured than is usual in the mass market. As a general principle, look for meat that is dark and dry to the touch, not pink and wet, with a veining of creamy white fat running through the meat that is known as 'good marbling'. Stewart buys a large rib joint of beef for his Sunday roast, which will feed five or six with enough left over for cold beef, chips and pickle on Monday evening. He favours the wing-rib joint, two ribs thick, from next to the sirloin – known as 'the butcher's cut' because it is often chosen by those in the know.
What I like about this way of dealing with the beef is its simplicity – no stuffing, barding or basting, just season the beef and whack it in until it is done.

Cooking Time

Stewart does not time the cooking of his beef exactly. Instead, he sticks a skewer into the centre when he thinks it is about ready. He 'reads' the temperature by putting the skewer on the end of his tongue or on his wrist. It should be just warm but not burning – 'a bit hotter than a baby's bottle,' he says – for meat that is nice and pink in the centre.

serves six, with some left over

50 g/2 oz lard, dripping or beef fat

salt and freshly ground black pepper

2.3–2.7 kg/5–6 lb joint of beef

1. Preheat the oven to 220°C/425°F/Gas mark 7.
2. Put a roasting tray with lard, dripping or, if your butcher will give it to you, the beef fat from the kidneys into the oven and let it melt until very hot.
3. To season the joint, put a small sprinkling of salt on the fat and pepper on the fat and flesh.
4. Put the meat in the oven and cook for 30 minutes.
5. Turn the oven down to 170°C/325°F/Gas mark 3 and cook for about a further 1¼ hours. As a general rule, per 450 g/1 lb allow 20 minutes for medium-rare and 15 minutes for rare beef. Then start testing, or, if you don't have confidence in the skewer technique, just give it another 20 minutes and you won't be far off.
6. Take meat out and leave to stand for at least 20 minutes, covered in foil to retain the heat.
7. An hour before the end of cooking you could put large chunks of peeled parsnips and potatoes around the joint to roast.
8. Serve with sweet onion gravy (recipe above), Italian-style roast potatoes, cauliflower cheese, sage and onion bread pudding (recipes follow) and a green vegetable.

Italian-style Roast Potatoes

Stewart follows tradition only up to a point. Instead of roasting potatoes in the fat around the joint, he now prefers to make Italian-style roast potatoes, cooked in olive oil and flavoured with basil, tomatoes and shallots.

serves five–six

1 kg/2¼ lb new potatoes, washed and left whole

150 ml/5 fl oz olive oil

4 shallots, peeled and quartered

salt and freshly ground black pepper

6 whole fresh basil leaves

3 fresh tomatoes, skinned, deseeded and chopped

1. Preheat the oven to 190°C/375°F/Gas mark 5.
2. Parboil the potatoes: put them in a pan of cold, well-salted water and bring to the boil. Boil for just 1 minute, remove from the heat and drain.
3. Return the potatoes to the saucepan, cover with a lid and shake to slightly roughen up the surface of the potatoes.
4. In the oven, heat the oil in a baking dish or roasting tray.
5. Add the potatoes and shallots to the oil and season with a little salt and pepper. Shake them around to coat with the oil and return to the oven.
6. After 30 minutes, add the basil and chopped tomatoes.
7. Return to the oven for 15–20 minutes, until browned.
8. Serve with the roast beef, or with any other meat or simply grilled fish.

Cauliflower Cheese

A traditional British dish with an Italian twist – Stewart uses mozzarella as well as Cheddar for extra bubble and stretch.

serves six

- *1 large cauliflower*
- *45 g /1½ oz butter*
- *salt and freshly ground black pepper*
- *1½ tbspn plain flour*
- *425 ml/¾ pint hot milk*
- *225 g/8 oz mature Cheddar, grated*
- *125 g/4 oz mozzarella cheese, sliced*

1. Remove the green leaves from the cauliflower and put to one side.
2. Place the whole cauliflower in a large pan of boilng salted water. Bring back to the boil. Simmer until just tender but not soft, testing with a knife. Drain properly in a colander for several minutes. (You could also cook the cauliflower in a large steamer.)
3. Meanwhile, make a roux: melt the butter in a saucepan, add a small pinch of salt and pepper. Add the flour and mix well. Cook for a couple of minutes, stirring, until lightly browned.
4. Add the hot milk slowly, a little at a time, stirring constantly.
5. Return to the heat, stirring, and bring to the boil. Allow to bubble for just a minute, then take off the heat.
6. Add the grated Cheddar to the sauce and stir until the cheese has melted.
7. Blanch the green leaves of the cauliflower in a pan of boiling water for just a few minutes, until tender but still bright and *al dente*.
8. Preheat the grill to high.
9. Place the whole cauliflower head in the centre of a heat-proof serving dish, arrange the strips of mozzarella cheese on top of the cauliflower and pour the sauce around it.
10. Brown the cauliflower under the grill (as far away as possible from the heat; a grill in an oven is ideal) until the mozzarella is bubbling and brown. Garnish the dish with the blanched green leaves spread out around the cauliflower.
11. Serve with roast beef and all the trimmings, or as a simple supper dish with toast or fried bread.

Roast beef ▶

Sage and Onion Bread Pudding

A variation on sage and onion stuffing which is crispy on the outside and soft inside.

serves four

1 x 170 g/6 oz packet sage and onion stuffing mix

110 g/4 oz diced ham or smoked bacon

1 medium onion, finely chopped

110 g/4 oz white breadcrumbs

30 g/1 oz butter

290–425 ml/½–¾ pint water

¼ medium onion, very finely sliced (optional)

1. Preheat the oven to 170°C/325°F/Gas mark 3 (or use the same oven as the beef when it is on this temperature for the second part of its cooking).
2. Make up the sage and onion stuffing as directed on the packet.
3. Gently fry the ham or bacon with the chopped onion in a little fat until the onion is softened and golden. Add to the stuffing with the breadcrumbs and mix well.
4. Grease a baking dish with half the butter. Put the stuffing into the dish and place in the bottom of the oven.
5. Cook for 1½ hours (or until the beef is ready), adding a little water at a time to ensure the mixture stays moist. Do not add any water to the side of the pudding for the last 20 minutes so the outside crisps up.
6. To serve, put the rest of the butter and thin slices of raw onion (optional) on top of the pudding. Serve with the roast and trimmings, or for supper with a fried egg on top.

Beef Stock

A great believer in the service, quality and flexibility of good local butchers, Stewart gets his meat and bones from his friend Kevin Laycock, a butcher in Horsforth, near Leeds. Kevin leaves a bit of meat on stock bones and also gives Stewart some marrow bone for a stock with a satiny smoothness.

Makes 1.7 litres/3 pints

2 large onions, roughly chopped
2 whole shallots
675 g/1½ lb beef bones and, if possible, a small marrow bone
2 carrots, thickly sliced
2 celery sticks, roughly chopped
2 leeks, roughly chopped
3 cloves of garlic
6 fresh sage leaves
a sprig of thyme
small (200 g/7 oz) tin of tomatoes
1 tbspn tomato purée

1. Place all the ingredients in a large stock pot.
2. Cover with water by about 1 cm/½ in. Bring slowly to the boil, skimming the surface to remove any scum that rises.
3. Simmer very gently, for 4 hours or longer, skimming occasionally.
4. Strain the stock of bones and vegetables, and strain again through a fine sieve (lined with muslin or a clean J-cloth). Let it cool and remove any fat from the top (easiest if you refrigerate the stock overnight).
5. Use in the onion gravy (recipe above) or freeze for use in soups and sauces another day.

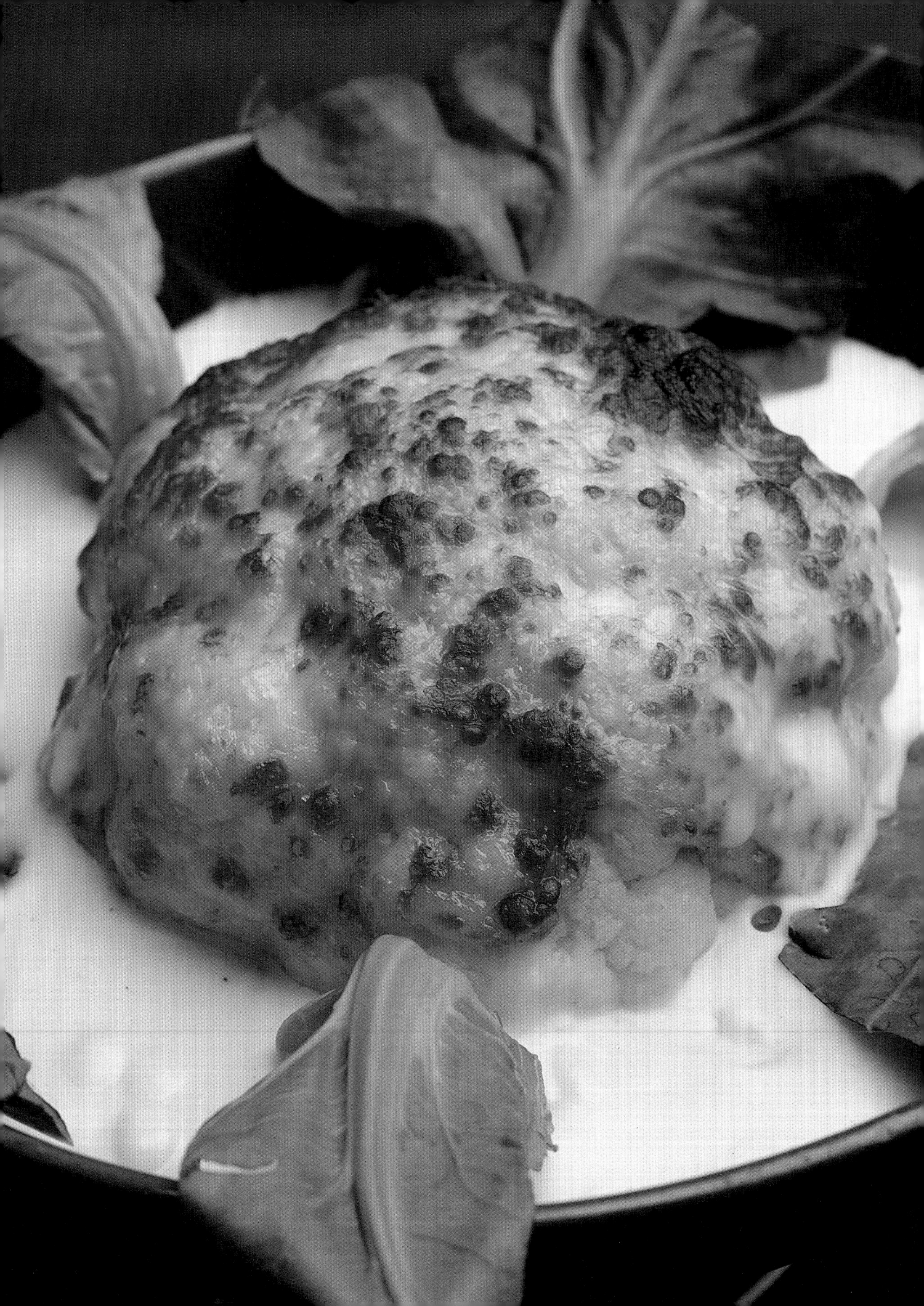

Boned and Stuffed Chicken

A good butcher will bone a chicken for you, given notice, or you can do it yourself at home with a sharp knife, a bit of practice and a lot of patience.

serves five–six

225 g/8 oz pork sausage meat

5 halves of tinned apricots (or 5 dried apricots if preferred)

6 fresh sage leaves, chopped

salt and freshly ground black pepper

1.8 kg/4 lb fresh chicken, boned

1 red pepper, roasted, skinned and cut into strips

1. Preheat the oven to 190°C/375°F/Gas mark 5.
2. Put the sausage meat, apricots and sage into a bowl and mix together. Season with salt and pepper.
3. Open out the chicken, skin side down, and season well with salt and pepper. Spread the stuffing in the chicken, pushing it into every cavity.
4. Place slices of roasted red pepper on top of the stuffing.
5. Neatly sew up the chicken, preferably using butcher's string (normal string can burn).
6. Roast in the oven, breast down, for 1 hour. Turn the bird every 15 minutes, cooking it first breast side down, then on one side, then the other, and finally breast up for the last 15 minutes. Pierce the thickest part with a skewer to check that the juices run clear and the meat is cooked.
7. Serve one or two thick slices per person with Italian-style roast potatoes (recipe above), green beans and carrots.

◀ Cauliflower cheese

RUMBLE IN THE JUNGLE

Felicity Keebaugh

MENU

Chicken and lemongrass soup

Squid with noodle and vegetable tentacles

Cointreau ice-cream

Many cooks (myself included) would credit the influence of their mothers in their culinary development – but not usually in the way that Felicity does. 'I started to cook,' she told me, 'because my mother's cooking was so *bad*. One day – I was probably about fourteen at the time – she opened a tin of tomato soup, added some sliced frankfurters and boiled it all up to a disgusting sludge. I thought, "Right, the time has come for me to take over in this kitchen." '

That was obviously a seminal moment because, while cooking with Felicity, it soon became clear to me that things get done *her* way. And it's not always the way you expect. Her cointreau ice-cream (see recipe below), for instance, is made in two parts, frozen separately, then whipped together in a Magimix and refrozen. 'It stops the acidity of the oranges curdling the cream,' she explained. Right. There may be other ways to achieve this, but I'm certainly not about to advocate them in Felicity's kitchen. And in the end her ice-cream is, of course, a triumph.

From this, and the other recipes below, Felicity's skills as a cook will be apparent. But it is her skills as a hostess that are perhaps most distinctive. Felicity has what you might call a pick 'n' mix urban social life, and a habit of ending up in unusual places with unusual people – often in the small hours of the morning. Out of these situations she collects, with her eclectic eye for charm and eccentricity, new friends. And then she invites them to dinner.

The five people she called up for the dinner we filmed had never met each other before (though they all had stories to tell about their hostess). 'They're all stars,' Felicity told me on the morning of the party. 'I'm guessing they're going to get on really well – the only danger is that there won't be room for them all to shine.'

There's hardly room to swing a cat in Felicity's north London council flat, let alone contain five orbiting egos – make that six, because, as all her guests agreed, Felicity is the biggest star of all. But by the time the first guest arrived, Felicity had transformed her little living room into a tropical jungle and she, in her skin-tight zebra-pattern miniskirt and bustière, was Tarzan and Jane all rolled into one.

Of all the dinners we filmed, this was probably the least known quantity. I felt it could be anything from a damp squib to an uncontainable explosion. In the end, it was neither of these extremes, but a thoroughly relaxed and entertaining evening, in which all her stars got a fair crack of the whip, and the dominatrix herself, who had said she was ready to break heads or stir things up as the situation demanded, hardly had to crack her whip at all.

My only regret was that during the entire proceedings I was stuck in Felicity's tiny kitchen like Cinderella, watching the pots and prepping the veg, while gales of lubricated laughter came wafting in from the table. The compensation? Well, I got to eat a fine plate of squid, which Felicity cooked for me specially, and, at the end of it all, a hug so big and busty that my ears are only just cooling down.

Thai Spaghetti Balls

Felicity serves these before dinner on the basis that guests who are expecting crisps will be surprised and pleased by hot hors d'oeuvres. These Thai balls, her own invention, are pretty surprising in their own right.

serves six as hors d'oeuvres

50 g/2 oz fideli or other pasta, such as thin spaghetti or linguini, broken into 8 cm/3 in pieces

125 g/4 oz mozzarella cheese, grated

handful of coriander leaves, roughly chopped

3 cm/1½ in square root ginger, very finely grated

handful of white breadcrumbs

2 eggs

1. Cook the pasta until it is *al dente*, then run cold water over it.
2. Mix everything together with the eggs and form into eighteen rough, two-bite-sized balls.
3. Heat some oil to 160°C/325°F in a large pan (or use a deep-fat fryer). Deep fry the balls until golden brown (about 2–3 minutes).
4. Serve hot, perhaps with a yoghurt dip flavoured with garlic and chopped mint.

Mini Mediterranean Bits

Mediterranean mini versions of quiches which go well with drinks – especially the sparkling Australian wine which Felicity insists her guests bring to dinner.

serves six as hors d'oeuvres

2 eggs

2 tbspn milk

50 g/2 oz ready-grated Parmesan cheese

freshly grated black pepper

50 g/2 oz butter, melted

4–6 sheets of filo pastry

6 green olives, stuffed with pimento, sliced thinly

4 sun-dried tomatoes, sliced thinly

2 shallots, finely diced

75 g/3 oz mature Cheddar cheese

1. Preheat the oven to 190 C/375 F/Gas mark 5.
2. Put the eggs in a blender. Add 2 tbspn milk, the Parmesan and plenty of pepper. Beat with a whisk or in a food processor to get a thin custard.
3. Lightly brush the 5–6 cm/2–2½ in diameter cups of a patty tray (or 7–8 cm/3–3½ in diameter individual tartlet moulds) with a little of the melted butter.
4. Brush two layers of filo pastry with melted butter and put on top of each other. Cut into two or three rough squares (depending on the size of both your patty tray cups and your filo sheets), to fit inside the cups, overlapping the edges slightly. Brush with more butter. Repeat to make six squares altogether.
5. Into each pastry-lined cup, put a few pieces of olive, a few slivers of sun-dried tomato, a little chopped shallot and a good teaspoon of grated Cheddar. Add the eggy mixture so it comes nearly up to the top.
6. Bake in the oven for 5 minutes until the egg mixture is lightly browned and the pastry is golden brown and crispy.

Chicken and lemongrass soup ▶

Chicken and Lemongrass Soup

Felicity reckons that there are few better ways to excite your guests at the beginning of a meal than with the taste explosions of a spicy Thai-style soup. It does require a few specialist ingredients (such as Thai fish sauce and lemongrass), but once you have these they're extremely simple to use and very rewarding. Felicity uses little marzipan cutters to make her version of Thai sculpted vegetables to float in the aromatic broth.

serves six as a starter

- *1 free-range chicken, 1 kg/2¼ lb*
- *1.5 litres/2½ pints water*
- *2 each of leeks, carrots and onions (plus any other stock vegetables you fancy)*
- *3 stalks of lemongrass*
- *4 cm/1½ in piece of ginger, peeled and finely sliced*
- *1–2 tbspn Thai fish sauce, to taste*
- *2 medium carrots, peeled*
- *6 tinned water chestnuts*
- *6 mint leaves*
- *18 coriander leaves*
- *1 red chilli, deseeded and finely sliced on the diagonal*
- *whites of 4 spring onions, finely sliced on the diagonal*

1 Cut the breasts off the chicken and reserve.

2 Make a good chicken stock with the rest of the chicken carcass by adding it to the water with the stock vegetables, bringing everything to the boil, lowering the heat and simmering very gently for at least 2 hours. Remove the carcass and vegetables and strain the stock through a sieve.

Optional: To get a sparkling clear soup, clarify the stock by adding the white and crushed shell of an egg to the stock while it is cool. Bring to the boil, whisking, and take off the heat. Strain through a sieve lined with muslin or a clean J-cloth. Repeat if necessary and you have the time.

3 Make 10 cm/4 in cuts down the lemongrass stalks to release their heat and flavour. Simmer the lemongrass and the ginger in the stock for 20 minutes and then remove.

4 Add Thai fish sauce to taste, taking care the broth does not become too salty.

5 Take the skin off the chicken breasts and cut the meat into thin strips. Stir-fry in a wok or non-stick pan in a little oil over a high heat until nicely browned.

6 Slice the carrots into very thin (2mm/⅛ in) discs and, using marzipan cutters or a knife, cut the carrots into tiny shapes. Cut the water chestnuts into three thin slices and then into shapes. Alternatively you could cut both vegetables into julienne strips. Put into the simmering stock, with the chicken pieces, for just a minute before serving. The vegetables barely need to cook and should retain their crispiness.

7 To serve, pour the soup into delicate Chinese soup bowls, making sure each serving has some vegetables and a few pieces of chicken. Finish each bowl with a single mint leaf, three coriander leaves, a few slices of chilli and some sliced spring onions.

Spicy Bell Pepper Salad

Mop up the oily juices of this colourful and piquant salad with plenty of good bread. Alternatively, use as a topping for bruschetta – grilled bread rubbed with garlic.

serves six as a starter or as part of a buffet

150–290 ml/¼-½ pint olive oil, according to taste

2 yellow peppers, deseeded and cut into long strips

2 red peppers, deseeded and cut into long strips

2 green peppers, deseeded and cut into long strips

5 cm/2 in square of ginger, peeled and cut into large cubes

2 large Spanish onions, sliced

4–5 whole dried red chilli peppers

2 cloves of garlic, peeled and roughly chopped

1 tspn caster sugar

salt and freshly ground black pepper

1. Put the olive oil in a large pan and add all the ingredients, apart from the sugar and seasoning. Count the cubes of ginger first (you are going to take them out).
2. Cook on a low heat, without a lid, for 45 minutes, until the peppers are soft and the oil is fragrant. Stir only very occasionally, to make sure nothing is catching on the bottom of the pan. Season with sugar, salt and pepper.
3. Leave to cool and take out the ginger and chillies before serving.
4. Serve at room temperature, perhaps surrounded by lettuce leaves such as radicchio or iceberg.

Squid with Noodle and Vegetable Tentacles

Always go to the main source is Felicity's philosophy in life and the same holds true in cooking, so she makes use of the diversity of ethnic shops in London. The fresh egg noodles and soy sauces used to make this come from a local Chinese store where the produce is fresh and cheap – and cooking tips come for free.

A Note on Buying Squid

Squid come in many sizes. Choose one, two or three per person according to size and your guests' appetites. Look for the small squid from the Mediterranean, sometimes called calamares which are about 8–12 cm/3–5 in long and very tender. If you can't get them, just buy the smallest fresh squid you can find. The fishmonger should clean them for you – ask for the body to be left whole. If the squid are on the large side, they may be tough. Felicity's Antipodean tip for tenderizing them is to put them in a plastic bag in the fridge with a mashed-up kiwi fruit for an hour.

serves six

250 g/9 oz fresh or dried egg noodles

3 tbspn thick sweet soy sauce

2 tbspn ordinary dark soy sauce

3 long, thin leeks

2 long red peppers

75 g/3 oz butter

salt and freshly ground black pepper

1 clove of garlic, finely chopped

6–18 small squid (depending on size), body only, kept whole

1 kiwi fruit (optional – see note above)

1 large, wide cucumber, peeled and very finely sliced on the diagonal

Thai sweet red chilli dipping sauce

1. If using dried noodles, blanch in boiling water for just a minute to tenderize. Soak the noodles in the thick and thin soy sauces for 20 minutes. They will start to turn a deep brown.
2. Transfer the noodles and sauce to a pan and heat gently for 5-10 minutes, turning once or twice (tongs are the best tool) and adding just a little water if they seem to be sticking together, until the noodles are a rich mahogany colour and tender.
3. Cut the leeks and the peppers into strips, as long and thin as possible. Cook in a steamer (or in a large saucepan with just a little water) until tender then add 30 g/1 oz butter, salt and pepper.
4. Melt 50 g/2 oz butter and add the garlic. Fry the squid for a few minutes. Timing depends on size and they will shrink as they cook.
5. Take six dinner plates, white if possible, and cover each with slightly overlapping layers of pale-green cucumber. Divide the squid between the plates, then twist the peppers, leeks and noodles together and put them all around, so they flow out as if in a swirl of multicoloured tentacles. Put a small cup of Thai sweet chilli dipping sauce in the centre of each plate.

◀ Squid with noodle and vegetable tentacles

Seven Vegetable Pie

Felicity describes this as 'a really serious pie' because it is no mean, brown vegetarian option but a cornucopia of vegetables, nuts and cheese.

serves six

- *1 medium aubergine, sliced*
- *75 g/3 oz butter*
- *1 onion, thinly sliced*
- *200 g/7 oz mushrooms, sliced*
- *6 medium potatoes, peeled and sliced*
- *2 carrots, cut in 6 cm/2½ in lengths*
- *2 courgettes, cut in 6 cm/2½ in lengths*
- *2 red peppers, de-seeded and cut into strips*
- *250 g/9 oz feta cheese*
- *300 g/11 oz ricotta cheese*
- *2 handfuls of sunflower seeds*
- *big handful of brazil nuts, roughly chopped*
- *6 sheets of filo pastry*
- *1 egg, beaten*

1. Salt the slices of aubergine and leave for 30 minutes. Rinse, drain, and squeeze as dry as possible in a clean tea-towel.
2. Fry the onion gently in butter until soft and lightly golden. Add mushrooms and fry lightly for a few minutes. Set the onion and mushroom mixture aside.
3. Fry the aubergine lightly in butter, so it takes on a little colour.
4. Parboil or steam the potato slices until not quite cooked. Lightly steam the carrots, courgettes and peppers (or stir-fry for a couple of minutes) so they are slightly tender but still crunchy.
5. Preheat the oven to 190°C/375°F/Gas mark 5.
6. Grease a deep baking dish with butter.
7. Line the dish with potato slices on the bottom and sides.
8. Mix together the carrots, courgettes, onion, mushrooms, feta, ricotta, sunflower seeds and brazil nuts.
9. Put a third of the vegetable and cheese mixture into the dish, on top of the potatoes, and pat down. Top with a layer of half the aubergines, then another layer of the vegetable and cheesey mixture, then the rest of the aubergines and the rest of the cheese and vegetable mixture.
10. Brush a sheet of filo pastry with melted butter, add the next sheet, brush with more butter and add another sheet. Keep going until you have a pile six sheets high. Put on top of the pie and cut the pastry to fit the shape of the pie dish if you want (it's fine for it to hang over the edges). Brush the top with beaten egg to glaze.
11. Cook in the oven for 30 minutes, until the pastry is golden brown.

Low-Fat Salad Dressing

This creamy-textured dressing goes well on a mixed salad of rocket, lamb's lettuce, cos lettuce, avocado, cucumber, apple and poached chicken. It will keep for a week in the fridge.

Shake well before each use.

1 small tub (125 g/4 oz) low-fat cottage cheese
2 tbspn apple juice
1 tbspn cider vinegar
4 leaves of fresh basil
a little fresh oregano

1. Put all the ingredients in a food processor.
2. Beat hard until the mixture is creamy and quite smooth.

Cointreau Ice-cream

Alcohol always features in at least one dish at Felicity's dinners. This ice-cream does not hold back on the Cointreau. Slosh on more at the end if you think your guests could use an extra kick. Felicity's trick for getting a smooth-textured ice-cream without using an ice-cream machine is to freeze the whipped cream and liquids separately, then whiz them together in a food processor.

serves six

570 ml/1 pint whipping cream
2 tbspn caster sugar
1 tspn vanilla essence
120 ml/4 fl oz Cointreau
225 ml/8 fl oz freshly squeezed orange juice (juice of 3–4 large juicy oranges)
12 physalises (Cape gooseberries)

1. Whip the cream until softly stiff. Stir in the sugar and vanilla essence. Put in a shallow plastic container and freeze.
2. In another plastic container, mix the Cointreau and orange juice and freeze.
3. Mix the cream and orange mixtures together in a food processor or by hand, then put back in the freezer until hard. Remove, mix together again and freeze once more.
4. To serve, make small ice-cream scoops using a melon baller. Pile up the scoops of ice-cream into smart glasses. Decorate each with two physalises (Cape gooseberries) and serve with long ice-cream sundae spoons.

Rambutan Ice-cream

This ice uses tinned rambutans but Felicity likes to decorate it with fresh rambutans if she can find them because she thinks they look like little hairy monsters.

serves six

2 x 400 g/14 oz tins rambutans

juice of 1 lime

approximately 2 tbspn sugar, to taste

3 eggs, separated

12 fresh rambutans to decorate (optional)

1. Drain the rambutans. Put in the food processor or liquidizer and process to a pulp.
2. Transfer to a mixing bowl and add the lime juice and sugar.
3. Beat the whites until stiff and fold into the rambutan purée.
4. Put the mixture in a plastic dish and freeze.
5. Put the frozen mixture in a food processor and beat up until it is slushy.
6. Add two of the egg yolks and beat until smooth. Return to freezer and leave until solid.
7. Remove about 30 minutes before serving, to soften slightly. Pile spoonfuls of the ice into glasses. Decorate with half-peeled fresh rambutans if you can find them.

Obscenely Rich Chocolate Cake

Adapted from a recipe from Felicity's cookery bible, Cookery the Australian Way. *The whole cake is so extremely rich that even very thin slices are more than enough. Serve with thick double cream for light relief.*

Cake base

200 g/7 oz soft butter

300 g/11 oz good chocolate (at least 55 per cent cocoa solids)

225 g/8 oz ground almonds

4 eggs, separated

100 g/4 oz caster sugar

Mousse topping

400 g/14 oz good chocolate

30 g/1 oz unsalted butter

½ tbspn vanilla essence

190–290 ml/⅓–½ pint double cream

6 eggs separated

1. Preheat the oven to 170°C/325°F/Gas mark 3.
2. Beat the butter in a food processor, or by hand, until pale and fluffy. Melt the chocolate in a double boiler or in a bowl over a pan of hot water.
3. Add the ground almonds, egg yolks, sugar and melted chocolate. Beat until well mixed. Turn out of the food processor into a large mixing bowl.
4. Whisk the egg whites until stiff and fold gently into the cake
5. Line a 23cm/9 in spring-form cake tin with greaseproof paper. Grease with butter.
6. Put the mixture into the cake tin and bake in the oven for 45 minutes - 1 hour, or until risen and firm.
7. Cool a little. Release from the tin and remove the paper lining. Cool on a wire rack.

To make the mousse topping

8. Melt the chocolate in a double boiler, or in a bowl over a pan of hot water, with the butter and vanilla essence.
9. Whip the cream until stiff.
10. Beat the egg yolks one at a time into the chocolate mixture. Fold in the whipped cream. Put in a bowl.
11. Whisk three of the egg whites until stiff. Fold into the chocolate mixture.
12. Spread the mousse on top of the cake base. Leave to set in the fridge.

Cointreau ice-cream ▶

GOURMET NIGHT

Gordon Irvine

MENU

Foie gras on malted bread
Quail's eggs in smoked salmon nests
with lime mayonnaise

Calvados sorbet

Haunch of wild boar roasted with herbs
and garlic in a red wine sauce
Garlic-glazed carrots
Buttercrust mashed potatoes
Puy lentils
French beans

A selection of French and Scottish cheeses

Passion fruit mousse in filo baskets
with a raspberry coulis and Cape gooseberries

An interest in cooking is not always keenly encouraged, or properly understood, by those around you. Among the Yarrow shipbuilders near Glasgow, where Gordon Irvine used to work as a marine fitter, cooking was generally something that the wives did at home. When Gordon turned up at work one day with some left-over spaghetti Bolognese and heated it up for his lunch, he was immediately the object of suspicion.

'They asked me, "Where d'ye buy that?" ' Gordon recalls, 'so I told them, "I never bought it, I made it", and someone said, "Were ye wearing a dress when ye made it?" So I said, "gi'us a kiss and ae'll tell ye..." '

Gordon may have had to endure a few weeks of leg-pulling, but pretty soon his workmates' sceptical humour had turned to genuine curiosity. 'After a bit they all wanted to taste my lunch, and it wasn't long before I was giving them recipes to take home for their wives.'

Now food is Gordon's quiet but all-consuming passion – an interest that seems to infiltrate every area of his life. He makes bread almost every day, and enjoys it the most when his two young sons, Andrew and David, help him knead the dough.

Gordon devotes a lot of his spare time to the pursuit and acquisition of the best ingredients and kitchen equipment. 'I remember when I first saw my big carving knife,' Gordon told me, 'in a catering suppliers in Glasgow. I went in and I touched it, and it was like Excalibur. I wanted that knife. So I went and put in some overtime and trotted back and bought the knife. It's so nice to use a well-weighted knife, and I think I appreciate it even more because I had to work for it.'

Gordon and his wife, Liz, love to travel in France, where holidays become an odyssey in pursuit of gastronomic excitement. 'What I like about it is that even the little things – like the bread or a simple salad – are always so good. And the big expensive things are pretty good too!'

It was on a recent trip to France that Gordon discovered foie gras – 'The first luxury food that I could really see the point of. Whatever you think of the way it's produced, the taste and texture are incredible – and the richness!'

Although Liz is also a very keen and competent cook (she excels at puddings, and the passion fruit mousse, even though Gordon made it, is her recipe), Gordon's extended family are definitely not so foody. 'They still think what we cook here is a bit peculiar, a bit fancy.' It's an on-going mission of Gordon's to challenge the palates of his family and friends, and this dinner was perhaps the greatest challenge to date.

The hardest nut to crack was going to be Gordon's brother-in-law Robert, who describes himself as 'a definite steak and chips man, me, well done, nice and crispy'. And, after reflection, 'I suppose I could eat a bit of lamb, but I don't much care for pork.'

Gordon had the novel idea of challenging Robert's conservative palate with a fine roast shoulder of wild boar – but not before he had sharpened his appetite with quail's eggs and foie gras. Robert didn't go a bundle on the goose liver, especially when he found out what it was, but Gordon scored a big hit when Robert said the meat was excellent – and therefore thought it must be steak!

Buying and Serving Foie Gras

Foie gras, the fattened livers of ducks and geese, is available in a number of forms in this country. The easiest to get hold of, and to serve, comes in tins or jars, either as a pâté (completely smooth and creamy) or 'en bloc' (a whole liver, in goose fat or jelly). These products are available in good delis and specialist food shops. Both are precooked, ready to eat cold straight from the tin or jar, and are best not tampered with. Serve with toast or warm bread, and a glass of well-chilled sweet white wine – ideally Sauterne. A slice placed on top of a grilled piece of fillet steak just before serving gives you a classic Escoffier dish, Tournedos Rossini.

For those prepared to look for it, a more adventurous product is a whole fresh liver, chilled and vacuum packed. This is what restaurant chefs prefer to buy, and what Gordon and I found in the warehouse. Although it has sometimes been part-preserved (or 'mis-cuit') by light salting and boiling in the bag, this product always needs further cooking. You could make your own terrine of the whole liver (and if you find a good recipe, it will be infinitely superior to anything you get from a tin). Or you could do what Gordon did and fry slices of it in a very lightly oiled pan for just half a minute each side. In this case, serve at once – ideally on lightly toasted rounds of Gordon's malted bread.

Foie Gras on Malted Bread

serves six people as a starter

2–3 slices malted bread per person (recipe follows)

225 g/8 oz fresh foie gras

1. Cut rounds out of the slices of bread with a 5 cm/12 in pastry cutter. Warm, but do not toast, under a grill.
2. Cut thin (approx 6 mm/¼ in thick) slices of foie gras.
3. Cook the foie gras for about 30 seconds each side in a dry frying pan. Pour off the fat as you go (keep this fat for flavouring sautée potatoes or other dishes).
4. Put a slice of foie gras on each round of bread.

◀ Quails' eggs in smoked salmon nests with lime mayonnaise

Malted Bread

Malted flour gives the bread a good flavour and texture. After years of using dried yeast, Gordon is now a convert to the fresh product and has persuaded Ross Dunbar's grocers in Neilston, seven miles from his home, to stock it for him. He uses this bread every day for his sandwiches. And for this dinner, little rounds of it were stamped out as bases for Gordon's 'amuse gueule' – slices of sautéed foie gras.

makes two loaves

1 tbspn sugar

425 ml/¾ pint lukewarm water

20 g/¾ oz fresh yeast

450 g/1 lb strong white flour

225 g/½ lb malted bread flour

30 g/1 oz lard

2 tspn salt

1. Mix the sugar with the warm water. Add the yeast and stir to dissolve it. Leave for 10 minutes until it gets a light frothy head, like a pint of beer.
2. Mix the two flours into a large bowl. Rub in the lard and stir in the salt.
3. Make a well in the centre of the flour. Pour in the yeast mixture and mix well.
4. When the dough becomes a sticky but workable mass (if it sticks too much to your fingers add a little flour), flour the work surface and place dough on it. Knead for 10 minutes until smooth.
5. Place dough back in the bowl and cover with a damp towel. Leave for between 45 minutes and an hour in a warm place (yeast is like a human: it does not perform well in cold, draughty places) until it doubles in size.
6. Grease and flour two 450 g/1 lb loaf tins. Knock back bread dough by turning it over on your hands four or five times.
7. Heat the oven to 250°C/500°F/Gas mark 9. Five minutes before putting the bread into the oven, place a tray of hot water at the bottom of the oven. This helps to get a good crisp crust on the bread.
8. When the bread has risen, put it into the oven, making sure there is enough space for the loaves to rise by another quarter. Cook at a high heat for 10 minutes. Reduce heat to 200°C/400°F/Gas mark 6 and cook for another 30 minutes.
9. Shape the dough into two loaves and put into loaf tins. Cover with a damp towel and leave for another 45 minutes to an hour, until it roughly doubles in size in the tin.
10. Remove the bread from the tins and tap the base of the loaves. They should sound hollow. If not, return them to the oven upside down on a wire rack for 5 more minutes. Remove and leave to cool.

Quails' Eggs in Smoked Salmon Nests

A very easy starter which looks special and is made a little unusual by the lime mayonnaise.

serves 6

12 fresh quails' eggs

170 g/6 oz smoked salmon cut into strips 6 mm/¼ in wide and 8 cm/3 in long

1. Put the eggs into a pan of boiling water and cook for 3 minutes. Drain and run under cold water to stop them cooking.
2. To peel, roll the eggs firmly but gently on the work surface to crack the shell all over. This makes them much easier to peel.
3. On a large white plate, arrange the smoked salmon strips into 12 small circular shapes, building them up in layers to make 12 little nests, each big enough to support one quail's egg.
4. Place a peeled quail's egg in the centre of each nest.
5. Top with lime mayonnaise (recipe follows) at the last minute.

Fresh Lime Mayonnaise

You could flavour a good ready-made mayonnaise with lime juice and zest if you do not want to make your own from scratch. When making home-made mayonnaise, all the ingredients should be at room temperature. If the egg or the oil is cold, the mayonnaise tends to split.

serves six

1 egg yolk

150 ml/¼ pint oil, half olive, half sunflower or groundnut

juice of half a lime

thinly grated zest of 1 lime

salt and freshly ground black pepper

1. Place the egg yolk in a mixing bowl and whisk with a balloon whisk (or an electric or manual hand whisk).
2. Mix in the oil very slowly, adding a very small trickle to start off with and slightly more at the end, whisking all the time.
3. Gradually whisk in the lime juice and half the lime zest
4. Season with salt and pepper to taste. Add more lime zest if desired.
5. Cover the mayonnaise and store in the fridge until ready to use.
6. Spoon the mayonnaise over the quails' eggs and smoked salmon nests. Do this at the last minute so it does not run or get a skin on it. This lime mayonnaise is also delicious with any hot or cold poached fish, especially salmon and sea bass.

Haunch of Wild Boar Roasted with Herbs and Garlic in a Red Wine Sauce

Gordon has eaten wild boar in France and Austria, where it is easier to find than in Britain. Some British farmers are now starting to produce it, though, and it is available by mail order and in specialist shops. A good butcher should be able to order it for you. It is a dense, flavoursome meat, which Gordon describes as a cross between beef and pork.

serves six

2–3 small onions, peeled and cut into quarters

2 large carrots, sliced

1 tbspn olive oil

1.3 kg/3½ lb from a haunch of wild boar

425 ml/¾ pint red wine

3 tbspn brandy

2–3 cloves of garlic, thinly sliced

chopped fresh herbs (small bunch of parsley, a few sprigs thyme and rosemary, 6 sage leaves)

salt and freshly ground black pepper

1. Preheat the oven to 190°C/375°F/Gas mark 5.
2. Put the onions and carrots into a roasting tin or terracotta 'chicken brick'.
3. Heat the oil in a heavy frying pan and brown the wild boar over a high heat on all sides until nicely coloured. Place the meat on top of the vegetables in the roasting tin or brick.
4. Pour off the fat from the frying pan and add the wine, scraping up the residue from the meat. Bubble for a couple of minutes to burn off the alcohol (otherwise it may taste bitter). Add the brandy and either flame it (easily done if cooking on gas by tippping the pan towards the flame until it catches) or boil it for a further 2 or 3 minutes.
5. Sprinkle the meat with garlic and herbs. Season with salt and pepper. Cover with foil and place in the preheated oven for 1 hour 20 minutes. Adjust the time according to the size of the joint, allowing 20 minutes per 450 g/1 lb plus 20 minutes. Keep basting or turn the meat over in its juices, roughly every half hour. Like pork, wild boar should be well cooked.
6. Twenty minutes before the end of the cooking time, remove the meat from the oven. Drain the juices into a bowl, separating off some (but not all) of the excess fat, and sieve the remaining juices into a pan. Put the meat back into the oven for a further 20 minutes, uncovered.
7. Take the meat out of the oven and rest, covered, for 10 minutes.
8. Boil the sauce to reduce it by roughly two-thirds to get a good, strong flavour. Check the seasoning and add more salt and pepper if needed.
9. Serve slices of wild boar with garlic-glazed carrots (recipe follows), buttercrust mashed potatoes (recipe follows), the reduced red wine sauce, Puy lentils and French beans.

Garlic-glazed Carrots

The unpeeled garlic gives a nice roasted garlic flavour to the carrots. You can eat the caramelized pulp of the garlic with the meat.

serves six

450g/1 lb carrots, peeled

3 tbspn olive oil

4–8 whole unpeeled cloves of garlic

salt and freshly ground black pepper

1. Cut the carrots in half if they are long, then lengthways into thin (3–4 mm/⅛ in) strips.
2. Blanch the carrots in boiling water for one minute, then drain and shake dry.
3. Heat the olive oil in a large frying pan and add the whole, unpeeled garlic cloves. Add the carrots and fry gently, turning occasionally, until nicely browned and tender.
4. Take the garlic and carrots out of the pan with a slatted spoon, shaking gently to remove excess oil. Season with salt and pepper.
5. Serve as an accompaniment to roast meats (especially boar, pork or lamb).

Buttercrust Mashed Potatoes

Gordon's variation on mashed potato sits nicely on a formal plate, but with a bit of cheese or chopped bacon stirred in before baking they make a lovely supper dish for a cold winter's day.

serves six

675 g/1½ lb floury potatoes (Gordon favours Golden Wonder or Kerrs Pinks), peeled and quartered

80 g/3 oz unsalted butter

six ramekins or non-stick muffin moulds

salt and freshly ground black pepper

1. Boil the potatoes in well-salted water until they are quite tender. Drain and leave in the sieve or colander for a few minutes to steam.
2. Put the potatoes back into a pan and place over a low heat. Mash thoroughly. When they are completely mashed and dry, add half of the butter.
3. Season with salt and pepper. Leave to cool completely.
4. Preheat the oven to 180°C/350°F/Gas mark 4.
5. With the remaining butter grease the base and sides of six ramekin dishes or non-stick muffin moulds. Fill the ramekins with mashed potatoes up to the top. Put a knob of butter on each of them, then put them on a baking tray near the top of the oven. Cook for 30 minutes or until they are golden brown and slightly puffed.
6. Loosen the potato from the edge of the ramekins and carefully turn out onto each plate.

Dijon Chicken

When Gordon is not trying out new tastes and techniques or converting his family to gastronomy, he likes simple French-inspired food such as this family supper dish.

serves four

50 g/2 oz butter

2 generous tspn Dijon mustard

4 chicken pieces, drumstick and thigh

4 handfuls fresh white breadcrumbs

1. Preheat the oven to 200°C/400°F/Gas mark 6.
2. Melt the butter and mix with the mustard.
3. Brush or spoon the mixture on to the chicken pieces.
4. Put the breadcrumbs on a plate and press the chicken into them so they coat the meat evenly.
5. Bake in the oven for around 40 minutes, or until the chicken is cooked. Pierce the thickest part of the meat with a knife to check that the juices run clear and the meat is cooked right through to the bone.
6. Serve with a couple of simple salads: tomato, olive oil and basil, and mixed green leaves.

Calvados Sorbet

Gordon likes to serve this as a pudding or between courses to clean the palate so that the flavours in the next course taste strong and fresh. In his menu, the idea was to cut through the richness and fatty aftertaste of the foie gras. Calvados is also a good digestif.

serves six

170 g/6 oz caster sugar
450 ml/16 fl oz water
thinly pared rind and juice of a large lemon
50 ml/2 fl oz Calvados
1 egg white

1. Heat the sugar and water in a saucepan over a low heat, stirring with a wooden spoon, until all the sugar has dissolved. Turn up the heat, bring to the boil and bubble rapidly for 5 minutes to get a light syrup.
2. Take the pan off the heat, add the lemon rind and juice, and leave to cool.
3. Pour the sugar syrup and Calvados into an ice-cream maker. While this is on, whisk the egg white until it is standing in soft peaks.
4. When the syrup is beginning to set in the ice-cream maker, fold in the egg white and return to the ice-cream machine for another 2-3 minutes. Pour into a container and put in the freezer. If making this by hand, put the mixture into a plastic container and freeze until it starts to set (30 minutes to an hour). Whisk the frozen edges back into the syrup and return to the freezer. Repeat the exercise and you should have a nicely slushy half-frozen mixture. Fold in the whisked egg white thoroughly and return the mixture to the freezer until completely hard.
5. If the sorbet is very hard, take it out of the freezer about 45 minutes before serving. You may not need to do this because the alcohol stops it from freezing too hard.

Passion Fruit Mousse in Filo Baskets with a Raspberry Coulis and Cape Gooseberries

This pudding, which is the creation of Gordon's wife, Liz, gives a fresh, fruity lift to the end of a meal when your appetite has started to weary. Gordon finds leaf gelatine easier to use than the powdered variety. He discovered some French passion fruit purée in his wholesale suppliers in Glasgow: it is certainly a useful short cut to scooping out a lot of passion fruits by hand. Filo pastry can be bought frozen in most good supermarkets. It is delicate stuff, but easy enough to deal with if you handle it according to the instructions on the packet. Most of all, keep it covered and do not let it dry out.

serves six

filo pastry baskets

6 sheets filo pastry
45 g/1[1/2] oz melted butter

1. Preheat the oven to 180°C/350°F/Gas mark 4.
2. Brush the pastry sheets with butter. Fold in four, buttering the pastry each time you fold it. Butter six heat-proof cup moulds or small ramekins, roughly 5 x 2 cm/2 x 1 in. They should be flat-bottomed if possible, such as dariole moulds.
3. Place in the preheated oven until golden brown (about 5 minutes). Keep checking on

the baskets after 3 minutes as they burn easily. Make the baskets in batches if you have only two or three suitable moulds.

4 Remove from the oven and carefully take the baskets off their moulds. Put back in the oven until crispy, right way up if the moulds are flat-bottomed or on their side if they are rounded. Remove from the oven and leave to cool on a wire rack.

mousse

2 x 3 g sheets gelatine leaf

170 g/6 oz passion fruit purée (pulp of 15–20 passion fruit)

approximately 1–2 tbspn icing sugar, to taste

170 ml/6 fl oz double cream

75 ml/3 fl oz crème fraîche

1 Cover the gelatine in cold water to soften.
2 Put the passion fruit purée into a bowl. Add icing sugar a little at a time, to taste. You can add little or none if you like it very tart.
3 Whip the double cream until stiff. Fold the crème fraîche into the whipped cream.
4 Fold the cream mixture into the passion fruit purée. Taste and add more icing sugar if desired.
5 Pour off water from gelatine leaf and melt the leaf in the microwave (full power for 30-40 seconds) or heat the soaked gelatine gently in a little water until it has dissolved.
6 Pour the melted gelatine into the mousse mixture, folding it in very briskly.
7 Pour the mixture into the filo baskets. Keep in the fridge to set the mousse (about 30 minutes).

raspberry coulis

450 g/1 lb fresh raspberries

2 dstspn caster sugar, to taste

1 Heat the raspberries and caster sugar in a saucepan. Bring to the boil so the juices run, then immediately take off the heat. Stir well to make sure the sugar has all dissolved.
2 Allow to cool, then pass through a sieve (a conical sieve is the easiest). Place in the refrigerator to keep cool.

to assemble puddings

1 Open up 24 Cape gooseberries and remove a third of the 'paper lantern' so the fruit can be seen and sits better on the plate.
2 Spoon a small amount of raspberry coulis and rotate the plate so the coulis runs round and covers the plate.
3 Place a passion fruit basket in the middle of each plate and decorate with one Cape gooseberry in each basket and three on each plate.

◀ Passion fruit mousse in filo basket with a raspberry coulis and Cape gooseberries

THE LAST SUPPER

Wynne Fearfield

MENU

Oysters
Shallot and chilli vinegar

Braised oxtail with celeriac
Mashed potatoes
Buttered cabbage

Rhubarb rice pudding

As you would expect in a series about home cooks, I came across a fair amount of passionate interest and excitement about food during my travels. But for sheer culinary obsession, Wynne was way ahead of the rest of the field.

Wynne cooks practically all the time, *even when there is nobody to feed*. As I write this, it's just after midnight, a time when most people are busy digesting – usually horizontally. But there is a very fair chance that right now Wynne is tinkering with her stock pots or adjusting the seasoning of some dish that will be finished tomorrow. And even if she has already retired, then you can bet the bedside light will still be on and she will be plotting future feasts in the company of one of her young men: Gary, Bruno, Raymond or Simon. (Wynne always refers to the authors of her favourite cookbooks by their first names – she feels she knows them so well.)

Wynne's obsession is driven by two things: a relentless curiosity about cooking and the desire to be very good at it – which she is, of course, but such is her self-deprecating nature that rarely does she ever produce anything which she can't find some tiny fault with. 'I know I am extreme,' she confessed to me. 'Sometimes a little globule of fat in my sauce will give me a breakdown. My daughter Francesca thinks I'm mad, I go on about food so much. But I can't bear for a dish not to work. I won't sleep, and then I'll get up the next morning and do it all over again, until I get it right.'

But while Wynne endures these culinary agonies, those who get to sample the products of her endless kitchen labours report regular helpings of ecstasy. The two most prolific consumers are her husband, Mike, an affable host who makes a fine job of tracking down wines to do justice to his wife's creations, and her neighbour Beryl, who benefits regularly from the frequent surpluses that result inevitably from Wynne's excessive enthusiasm.

Mike, who gets a restaurant-calibre three-course meal (often with two different puddings!) almost every night of the week, says he is now resigned to the inevitability of a bit of middle-age spread: 'But I can't think of a nicer way to earn it.' Beryl talks excitedly about the little food parcels that Wynne leaves for her on the window-sill: 'You never know what it's going to be, but it's always something unusual that I probably wouldn't cook at home. And,' she adds, with enormous sincerity, 'always such *depth* of flavour.'

On the morning of the dinner, while munching her toast, Beryl suffered an unusual piece of bad luck: she lost the crowns on her front two teeth. It's surely a testament to Wynne's cooking that even on a Sunday Beryl managed to track down a dentist to fix her up, so that by the evening she was fully toothed again and ready to do battle with four courses of Wynne's finest food.

The sad news is that Mike and Wynne are moving away. This dinner was a farewell to friends and neighbours, by whom Wynne's cooking and Mike's hospitality will be sorely missed. For those of us who would like an occasional reminder of the light burning in her kitchen into the small hours, her excellent recipes appear below.

Oysters on Ice

Wynne loves the look, taste and texture of oysters. A gastronomic myth runs that they are best swallowed whole straight away, but it is far better to let them linger a while – a good couple of chews at least. Serve them on ice with a chilli and shallot vinegar, quartered lemons, Tabasco or simply in their own juices, and with quarters of lightly buttered brown or rye bread.

How to Open Oysters

Opening oysters is hard work until you are very practised. Hold the oyster in one hand in a cotton cloth (for protection and a firm grip), deep side down, flat side up, so the oyster stays in the deep half of the shell, retaining as much juice as possible. Insert the end of a short-bladed stiff knife (or dedicated oyster knife) just to one side of the shell hinge. Push into the oyster shell, then pull back across the underside of the top (i.e. flat) half of the shell, thereby – you hope – releasing it.

Discard the top half of the shell and serve the oyster in the bottom half. Some people release the meat from where it is attached to the shell and turn the oyster over, but I think it looks better and stays fresh longer if you leave it attached.

serves six

18 rock oysters
18 native oysters
enough ice-cubes to fill a serving bowl
3 lemons, quartered
seaweed for decoration (optional)

1. Open the oysters (see above) and store on their half-shells in the fridge.
2. Crush several trays of ice by putting the cubes in a plastic bag and bashing with a rolling pin.
3. Serve the opened oysters on plenty of crushed ice with quartered lemons, Tabasco, shallot and chilli vinegar (recipe follows) and brown bread and butter.

Shallot and Chilli Vinegar

If this is made a day or two in advance, the flavours will mingle and improve. It will keep for weeks.

serves six

150 ml/5 fl oz red wine
300 ml/10 fl oz red wine vinegar
4 shallots, peeled and finely diced
2 red chillies, seeded and finely diced

1. Mix all the ingredients together.
2. Serve in ramekins or small bowls with the oysters.

Note: A few drops on each oyster is plenty

Oysters on ice ▶

Stocks

Tips for successful stock-making

Before she did her course at Leith's, Wynne was pretty handy with a stock cube. Now she believes that good fresh stocks are the cornerstone of good cooking, and there'll be a stock pot bubbling gently on the back burner most days of the week.

Wynne's precise stock recipes below produce excellent results, but it is worth bearing in mind that recipes for stock are infinitely variable, and will depend on what bones and vegetables come to hand. When improvising your own stocks, it is worth bearing in mind a few simple guidelines:

• Browning the bones and vegetables helps to give colour and flavour when making veal or beef stock. Do not burn them or the stock will be bitter.

• Very gentle simmering – just a few bubbles rising to the top – and regular skimming are vital for a clear, clean stock. Keep removing all the impurities from the top of the liquid. Once the froth is a clean white rather than a dirty brown, you can stop skimming unless you want a clear stock.

• Gelatinous cuts and bones such as oxtail, knuckles, pigs' trotters and beef shin give maximum flavour to beef and veal stocks. For a really rich chicken stock, use a boiling fowl, which can then be eaten as a meal with vegetables.

• The classic vegetable flavourings for stock are onions, carrots (both essential to give sweetness), celery, parsley, black peppercorns and bay leaves. Unpeeled onions give good colour to chicken stock. Leeks or leek tops, spring onion trimmings, parsnips (just a half) and celeriac (a small nugget) are some optional extras.

• The flavour of meat stock improves with long, slow simmering. Wynne ideally likes to simmer beef or veal stock for up to 6 hours and chicken stock for 3 hours. Fish stock, however, should be simmered for 30 minutes maximum or it can become bitter.

• Store stock by freezing it in plastic containers. Reduce the stock by straining it through muslin or a clean J-cloth, then boiling it hard until it halves in volume to make it easier to store. You can reduce it down further until it is just a couple of centimetres deep in the pan and quite syrupy in texture. This jus has a good, concentrated flavour (the home cook's equivalent of Marmite) and is delicious when added to pasta, vegetables or sauces.

Veal Stock

makes 2 litres/3½ pints

1 kg/2¼ lb veal bones, chopped into small pieces

450 g/1 lb chuck steak or shin of beef, roughly chopped

1 tbspn vegetable oil

3 carrots, peeled and chopped

2 onions, peeled and chopped

3 celery sticks, chopped

1 tbspn tomato purée

4 cloves of garlic, crushed

6 large, flat-topped mushrooms

1 wine glass red wine

1 wine glass white wine

2.5 litres/4 pints water

4 sprigs of thyme

1 bay leaf

6 black peppercorns

1. Preheat the oven to 220°C/425°F/Gas mark 7.
2. Roast bones for about 20–30 minutes in the oven in a little oil until evenly brown (but not burnt), shaking them around occasionally or turning them with tongs. Then transfer to a large stock pot.
3. While the bones are roasting, brown the meat in a frying pan over a high heat in the oil, then add to the bones in the stock pot. In the same pan fry the carrots, onion and celery over a medium heat until golden. Add the tomato purée and garlic. Fry, stirring, until the garlic has lightly coloured. Then transfer to another dish and set aside.
4. In the same frying pan, colour the mushrooms in a little oil and add to the vegetables. Deglaze the pan with the wines. Boil until reduced by about half, then add to the bones and vegetables in the pot.
5. Cover the bones and meat in the stock pot with the water. Bring slowly to the boil, skimming off any grey-brown scum that rises to the top. When the scum is a clean white colour you can stop skimming, unless you want a clear stock.
6. Add the vegetables, bay leaf, peppercorns and reduced wine to the bones and bring back to the boil. Simmer slowly for 5 to 6 hours, skimming occasionally.
7. Lift the bones from the pan. Tip the rest of the stock into a fine sieve over a large pan. Strain again through a fine sieve or, better still, muslin or a clean J-cloth.
8. Reduce the stock down by boiling, if you want to make it easier to store.
9. Once the stock is cool, put in the fridge to chill. The fat will rise to the top and set firm and can be easily lifted or scraped off the jellied stock in one or two pieces.

Chicken Stock

makes 2 litres/3½ pints

2 kg/4½ lb chicken wings, 2 whole chicken carcasses, or a 2 kg/4½ lb boiling fowl

2 onions, quartered, skins left on

2 carrots, quartered

parsley stalks, slightly crushed

4 sprigs of thyme

1 bay leaf

6 white peppercorns

2.5 litres/4 pints water

1. Put all the ingredients into a large stock pot.
2. Cover with the water. Bring slowly to the boil, skimming off the fat and scum as you go. Simmer gently for 3 hours, skimming frequently.
3. Remove the stock pot from the heat. Strain the stock through a fine sieve and allow to cool.
4. Put in the fridge, preferably overnight. Remove all the fat which congeals on top of the cold stock.

Fish Stock

This is a sophisticated way of making fish stock. If you want a simpler method, simply add the vegetables to the fish bones and water without sweating them in butter first. Wynne likes to use turbot and brill trimmings if possible.

Makes 1 litre/ 1¾ pints

- *1 tbspn vegetable oil*
- *a small onion, roughly chopped*
- *1 leek, white part only, diced*
- *1 stick of celery*
- *a few fresh herbs such as parsley, chervil and a little tarragon*
- *290 ml/½ pint white wine*
- *900 g/2 lb white fish bones and heads, rinsed to get rid of any blood*
- *6 white peppercorns*
- *½ bay leaf*
- *1.2 litres/2 pints water*

1. In a pan, sweat the vegetables and the herbs in a little vegetable oil until they are soft but not coloured.
2. Add the wine and let it boil down to a fifth of its original volume to get a good intensity of flavour.
3. Add the fish trimmings, peppercorns and half bay leaf.
4. Add the cold water and bring almost up to the boil.
5. Just before the water comes to the boil, skim the stock and turn it down. Simmer for 20–30 minutes maximum, any longer and it can become bitter.
6. Cool the stock and then pass it through a fine sieve or a sieve lined with muslin.
7. Once the fish and vegetables have been removed, you can reduce down the stock for a stronger flavour or to make it easier to store.

Mussel and Saffron Soup

A beautiful saffron-gold soup using Wynne's good fish stock.

serves four

- *1.35 kg/3 lb mussels*
- *100 g/4 oz butter*
- *1 shallot, sliced*
- *120 ml/4 fl oz white wine*
- *a few parsley stalks, bruised*
- *freshly ground black pepper*
- *450 g/1 lb leeks, sliced*
- *1 medium onion, chopped*
- *15 g/½ oz flour*

1. Scrub the mussels and remove the beards. Discard any which are cracked or do not close when they are tapped.
2. Melt a quarter of the butter. Sweat the shallot in the butter until it is soft but not coloured.
3. Add half the wine and the parsley stalks.
4. Add the mussels and a few grinds of black pepper. Put a tightly fitting lid on the pan and cook the mussels for about 3 minutes, shaking occasionally, until they are open. Discard any which do not open.
5. Strain the mussels through a sieve, ideally lined with muslin, reserving the liquor.
6. Melt the remaining butter and cook the leeks and onion over a medium heat for about 5 minutes, until they are soft and have take up a little colour.

◀ Braised oxtail with celeriac

570 ml/1 pint fish stock

salt

a little saffron

2 tbspn crème fraîche

a little flat-leaf parsley, chopped

7 Sprinkle on the flour and cook, stirring occasionally, for 3–5 minutes to cook off the raw flavour of the flour.

8 Add the remaining wine, the fish stock and the mussel liquor. Season with salt and bring to the boil.

9 Add a pinch of saffron. Turn the heat down and simmer the soup for 20 minutes. Liquidize and sieve.

10 Meanwhile, take the mussels out of their shells and discard the shells (or you could keep a few back for a garnish). Add the mussels to the soup. Check the seasoning. Reheat the soup, but do not boil.

11 Stir the crème fraîche into the soup and garnish with a little chopped flat-leaf parsley.

Braised Oxtail with Celeriac

Wynne has around 300 cookbooks. This recipe is based on one from her trusty manual, Leith's Cookery Bible, *by Prue Leith and Caroline Waldegrave.*

serves six

2.7 kg/6 lb oxtail cut into pieces (the butcher will do this)

flour seasoned with salt and freshly ground black pepper

30 g/1 oz beef dripping or 2 tbspn oil

340 g/12 oz carrots, peeled and thickly sliced

225 g/8 oz onion, peeled and sliced

150 ml/5 fl oz red wine

570 ml/1 pint veal or beef stock

4 sprigs of thyme

1 bay leaf

½ tspn caster sugar

½ tspn tomato purée

juice of ½ lemon

salt and freshly ground black pepper

1 Preheat the oven to 150°C/300°F/Gas mark 2.

2 Toss the tail pieces in the seasoned flour. Fry in the dripping until well browned on all sides. Drain in a colander.

3 Brown the carrots and onions. Take care not to burn the vegetables or you may introduce a bitter note to the taste of the dish.

4 Add the oxtail, wine and stock, then add the thyme, bay leaf, sugar, tomato purée, lemon juice, salt and freshly ground black pepper.

5 Bring just to the boil, cover and put into the oven to braise for 4–5 hours until tender.

6 When the meat is cooked and falls easily off the bone, remove the vegetables and meat from the pan with a slotted spoon. Put the meat in the fridge to chill and discard the vegetables.

7 Push the sauce through a sieve into a pan. Boil to reduce down if necessary (it depends on how strong you want the sauce to be). Check the seasoning after reducing the sauce.

8 Remove the fat from the chilled oxtail and take the meat from the bones in chunky pieces.

9 Preheat the oven to 180°C/350°F/Gas mark 4.

10 Place the oxtail meat in six dariole moulds or ramekins, and spoon over a little of the sauce to moisten. Put in a roasting tin, filled with enough hot water to come three-quarters of the way up the sides of the moulds. Put the meat in the oven to heat through for 20 minutes.

11 Meanwhile, fry the celeriac cubes in a little oil for about 5 minutes or more, until evenly browned.

To accompany and garnish

900 g/2 lb celeriac, peeled and cut into 2 cm/1 in dice

2 tbspn chopped parsley

2 tbspn chopped chives

12 To serve, place a mound of oxtail on to each plate, pour the sauce around, scatter around the celeriac and scatter over chopped parsley and chives. Serve with mashed potatoes and buttered cabbage or greens (recipes follow).

Mashed Potatoes

After experimenting with dozens of ways of making mash, Wynne has settled on the painstaking method of pushing the potatoes through a sieve with a wooden spoon to get a fine, silky-smooth purée. A mouli-légumes also works for this purée but never use a food processor, as it will break down the starch and make the potatoes gluey. Wynne uses unsalted butter and occasionally olive oil or butter mixed with an egg yolk for added richness but shuns milk, which, she says, produces a less good taste and a runny texture. Wynne's top spud for mash is Desirée, followed by (in no particular order) Romano, Cara, Estima, King Edwards, Marsona, Elvira, Pentland Squire, Maris Piper or Bintje.

serves six

900 g/2 lb Desirée potatoes, peeled and cut into quarters

100 g/4 oz unsalted butter

salt and freshly ground black pepper

1. Put the potatoes in a pan of salted cold water. Bring to the boil and simmer until tender. Do not boil too hard as this often makes the potatoes disintegrate or leaves the centre hard when the outside is cooked.
2. Drain the potatoes in a colander and let them dry for a couple of minutes.
3. Purée the potatoes through a sieve or mouli-légumes into a clean saucepan. Add the butter. Heat gently so the butter melts and can be stirred into the potato. Season with salt and pepper.

Buttered Cabbage or Greens

Serve these with the oxtail. The outer green leaves of cabbage, especially a good cabbage like savoy or primo, have much more flavour than the pale inner ones (which can be set aside and used for coleslaw). Wynne's other tip is not to overcook them and shred them too fine, otherwise there's nothing to bite.

serves six

675 g/1½ lb spring greens or green cabbage leaves, trimmed of tough stalks and shredded into 2 cm/1 in slices

30 g/1 oz unsalted butter

salt and freshly ground black pepper

1. Blanch the shredded cabbage in boiling salted water for 2 minutes. Drain well.
2. Fry the cooked cabbage in the butter for just a minute or so, until it becomes glossy. Season with salt and pepper.

Rhubarb Rice Pudding

Wynne's husband, Mike, said he loathed rice pudding. But Wynne has always loved it so in an attempt to convert him she consulted her cookbooks for three modern and delightful variations on the nursery food classic. I had to help her choose between them for her dinner and it wasn't easy. After happily guzzling all three, I plumped for the rhubarb version.

This recipe is adapted from Rhodes Around Britain *by Gary Rhodes.*

serves four–six

50 g/2 oz unsalted butter

450 g/1 lb rhubarb, cut into 3 cm/1½ in pieces

100 g/4 oz caster sugar

100 g/4 oz short-grain pudding rice

570 ml/1 pint milk

50 g/2 oz caster sugar

4 egg yolks

150 ml/5 fl oz double cream

1 tspn per ramekin demerara or caster sugar

1. Heat the oven to 180°C/350°F/Gas mark 4.
2. Melt half the butter in a pan and add the rhubarb and the 100 g/4 oz caster sugar. Cook on a high heat for about 4 minutes. Stir occasionally but take care not to break up the rhubarb.
3. Drain the rhubarb through a sieve, reserving the juice, then spoon the rhubarb into ramekins, filling each about one half full.
4. Put the rice in a saucepan, cover with cold water and bring to the boil. Drain and rinse with cold water.
5. Bring to the boil three-quarters of the milk, 25 g/1 oz caster sugar and the rest of the butter in a pan.
6. Add the rice. Bring back to the boil and simmer for about 10 minutes, until the rice is *al dente*.
7. Beat the egg yolks and remaining sugar together. Boil the cream and remaining milk and pour on to the yolks, stirring. Mix with the rice and the reserved rhubarb juices.
8. Spread the rice mixture on top of the rhubarb, almost to the top of each ramekin.
9. Stand the ramekins in a baking tray filled with hot water and bake in the preheated oven for about 30 minutes, until the mixture is set but still slightly wobbly.
10. Remove from the baking tray and leave to go completely cold. Chilling in the fridge will help to prevent the mixture from bubbling up.
11. To make a crème brûlée topping, sprinkle a thin, even layer of demerara or caster sugar over the top of each ramekin. Glaze with a blow torch or put under a very hot grill until the sugar is melted and lightly browned.
12. Serve hot or cold. For an alternative presentation (see picture), do not give the rice puddings a brûlée top or layer on top of drained rhubarb, but turn them out onto plates and serve surrounded by a sauce made from sieved rhubarb.

Two presentations of rhubarb rice pudding ▶

HOG HEAVEN

Fred Carr

MENU

Spit-roasted pork
Dried fruit stuffing
Crackling
New potato and herb salad
Three pepper salad

Brownies and ice-cream

Not everybody has the courage or the confidence to drive home from the local butcher with a whole dead pig in the boot of the car. But two or three times a year London stockbroker and Gloucestershire weekender Fred Carr does just that. *Why?*

'Well,' says Fred, with a genial grin, 'mainly because there's a good gang of assorted Gloucestershire drunks and villains whom I like to have over here once in a while, especially when the sun's shining, and a whole spit-roast pig seems like a good way of feeding the lot of them without too much hassle.'

But somehow the idea of spit-roast pig as convenience food doesn't quite ring true. And in the day I spent with Fred at his unfeasibly pretty rambling Cotswold farmhouse I soon realized there was a little more to his porcine party piece than just bunging a pig over a giant barbecue to feed the masses. The mounting, stuffing, stitching, turning, basting and roasting of a 70-lb porker is major undertaking, a day-long project, no less.

It may not seem the obvious way for a hard-working City executive to unwind at the weekend, but pressed on the matter, Fred admits that for him, the spit roast really is relaxation – maybe even therapy: 'Whether I'm at home or at work, I like to have a project. And I think I like the spit roast because you have to concentrate hard on what you're doing. And I guess I prefer big things to small things. You know, when I was a boy I did a bit of model-making, but I didn't want to make a small model aeroplane, I wanted to make a bloody great thing with a 6-foot wing span!' As one of his friends put it later at the party, 'Fred's the kind of cook who would rather stuff a pig than a mushroom.' Quite.

When he goes to work on the pig, Fred is a charming and slightly paradoxical combination of gung-ho enthusiast and perfectionist. 'I really want to get the blanket stitching right this time,' he told me. 'Because last time I made a bit of a pig's ear of it. With all due respect,' he added, slapping the rump of the long pink beast stretched out on his dining-room table, awaiting stuffing.

What I found most challenging, and also most enjoyable, about the process was the number of skills called upon during the course of the day, from the sewing up of the stuffed beast (to which there is a knack I have yet to master), right through to the building up of the fire in pursuit of perfect all-over crackling.

And when we finally got to eat the pig, some twelve hours after we'd first set to work, I was immediately reminded that this was not just a logistical exercise. For flavour, succulence, outstanding crackling and a subtle hint of real wood-fire smokiness, Fred's pig knocked the stuffing out of any pork I've had from a domestic oven.

This is not the kind of cooking that is going to appeal to everybody. For a start, you have to be a fairly committed carnivore. But at the end of the day (and it's a long day) job satisfaction corresponds to the scale of the operation: it's absolutely huge!

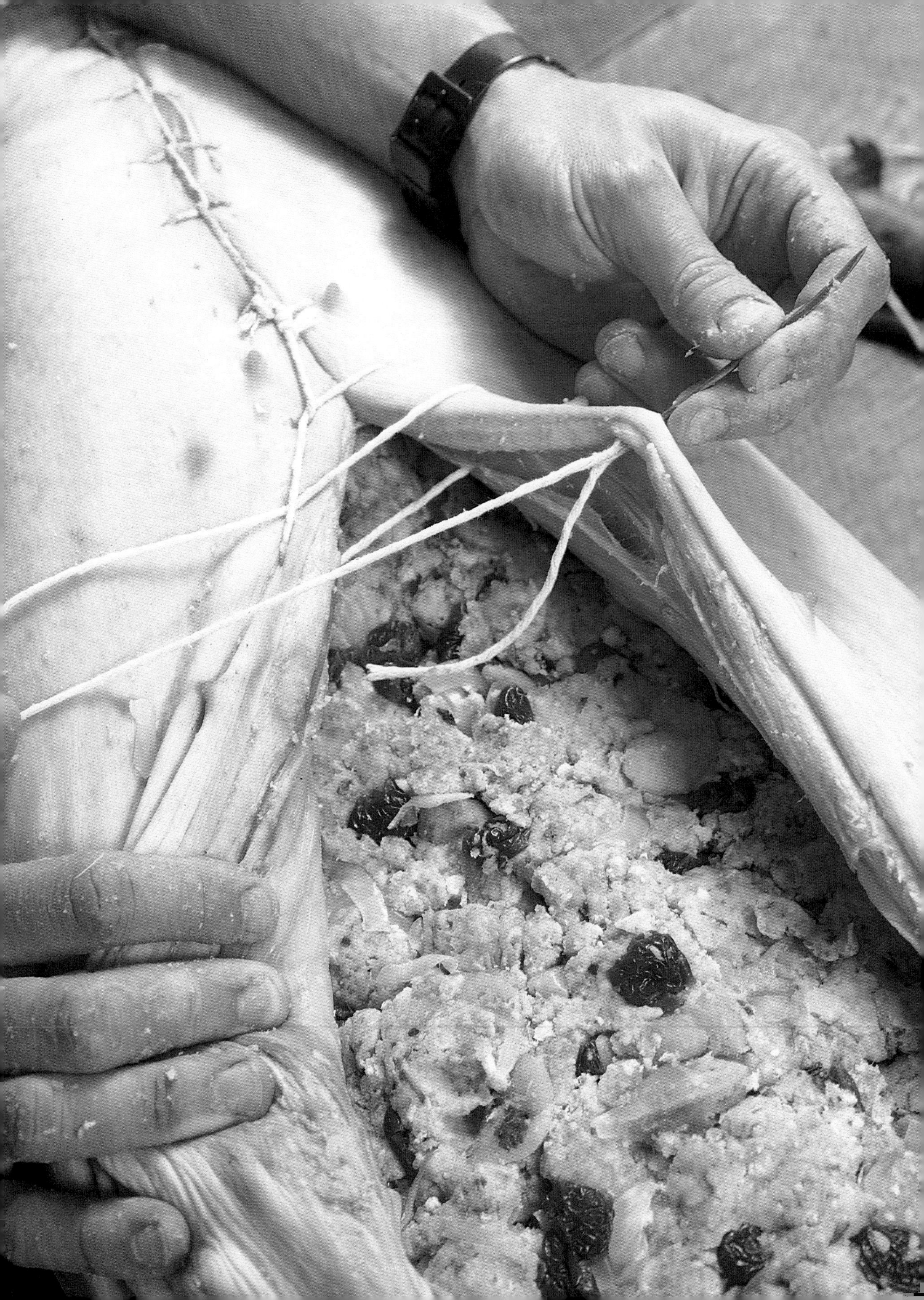

Hog Roast

What follows is designed to be a complete guide to stuffing and spit-roasting a whole pig at home. It is, I think, a very exciting and satisfying culinary challenge, and the end results – succulent, flavourful meat with a wonderful wood-smoky taste – make it all worthwhile. Remember, however, that only practice makes perfect. A spit-roasting kit is an investment so don't be downhearted if it doesn't all go like clockwork the first time.

Choosing Your Animal

To feed at least fifty hungry guests, Fred roasts a medium-sized pig, around 32 kg/70 lb in weight once gutted. He orders this specially, at least a month in advance. Spit-roasting a pig is for the ambitious, because it is so large and takes so long to cook. Fred suggests that the beginner starts with a whole lamb, which takes half the time to cook – and is easier to carry!

Spit roasting out of doors tends to be a summer activity (though the roasting fire would certainly keep you warm on a winter's day) and if the weather is hot, some consideration should be given to the question of storage. You don't want your beast hanging around for too long in a warm place. A whole pig is never going to fit into your fridge, so your best option is to pick it up from the butcher on the morning of the day you intend to roast it – that way you will be dealing with it almost as soon as you get it home. If that's not practical and you have to pick it up the day before, keep it overnight in the coolest part of the house: cellar, larder or, in Fred's case, the bathtub! Don't keep it for any longer than is necessary, and certainly not for more than one night.

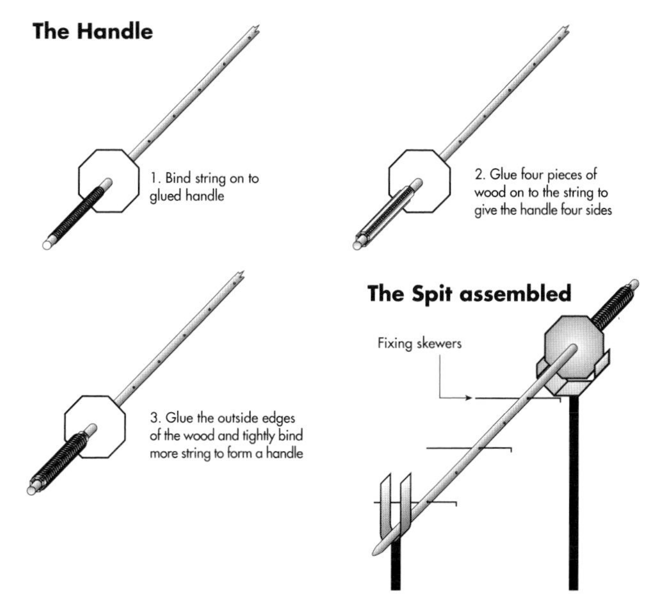

◀ Sewing up the pig with a good blanket stitch (stage three)

Stage One: Making the Stuffing

Every time he roasts a pig, Fred varies the ingredients and quantities for his stuffing. The constants are good sausage meat, breadcrumbs, onions and a variety of dried fruits. The important thing is to have enough – or rather, to be on the safe side, slightly too much. Incidentally, if your maths is up to it, you could scale this recipe down by a factor of 20 for a delicious stuffing for a leg or loin of pork.

serves fifty

a small whole pig (approximately 32 kg/70 lb), gutted and cleaned (but the kidneys can be left in)

300 g/11 oz dried mangoes

500 g/1 lb 2 oz dried sour cherries

500 g/1 lb 2 oz dried apricots, halved

8–10 medium onions, roughly sliced

675 g/1½ lb (2–3 tins) pitted prunes, drained and halved

the same amount by volume of white breadcrumbs (c. 3 or 4 large loaves)

c. 3 kg/7 lb Cumberland (or any good quality) sausage meat

2 tspn salt and plenty of freshly ground black pepper

big handful of fresh thyme, chopped

1 very large bucket for mixing

1. Soak the dried mangoes, cherries and apricots for a few hours, or preferably overnight. Drain and chop roughly.
2. Mix the onions with the dried fruit and prunes in a large bucket.
3. Add the breadcrumbs and mix thoroughly with a clean pair of hands.
4. Crumble the sausage meat into the bucket and mix thoroughly, making sure that the breadcrumbs do not collect at the bottom of the bucket. Season well with salt and pepper and add the thyme. Go on mixing until all the ingredients are thoroughly combined.

Stage Two: Mounting the Pig on the Spit

A spit for an animal of this size is not something you can easily improvise. Fred's first-ever spit was a gadget he picked up from a second-hand catering shop in London which was not designed for the purpose. When his improvisations did not work, Fred devised and made his own contraption, which he later got a local blacksmith to copy. If you know a proficient metal-worker or blacksmith, you could do the same, but bear in mind the important features outlined *on p. 107.*

You can also get an excellent spit kit made up to order from Tom Faulkner Designs, 13 Petley Road, London W6 9SU. Tel. 0171 610 0615. Fax 0171 386 0797.
Alternatively, you can hire a gas-fired motorized spit from various catering companies. This takes the elbow work, a large part of the judgement and some of the flavour out of the process and therefore makes the whole thing less of a challenge. Fred would not approve, but if you're interested, try Yellow Pages under Catering Companies.

Equipment

1 spit kit, comprising:

2 forked steel or iron supports

1 heavy iron or steel spit

3 steel fixing skewers

The supports

You make two holes in the ground at either end of the fire (about 1.8 metres/6 feet apart, depending on the size of the pig), using a large spike and a sledgehammer. Slot the forked supports into these holes so an animal suspended from the spit is around 60 cm/2 feet above the ground at its lowest part. One support is a simple fork, the other is shaped to receive the octagonal turning plate at the handle end of the spit (see close-up photo).

The spit

The spit is the load-bearing spike that goes through the pig from head to tail. It should be at least 2.1 metres/7 feet long, and 2.5 cm/1 in in diameter, with holes drilled through at 30 cm/1 foot intervals to receive the skewers, which help hold the pig on the spit. At one end it should have a non-heat conductive handle (usually wood wrapped with string) and an octagonal turning plate. This allows the spit to be turned to eight different positions, ensuring good all-round cooking.

The fixing skewers

These go through the pig at right angles to the spit to stop the beast slipping when the handle of the spit is twisted. They should be pointed at one end, about 45 cm/18 in long and 6 mm/¼ in in diameter, and go through the sides of the pig, passing through the holes in the spit.

Procedure

1. Lay the pig on its back on a table. Push the pointed (i.e. non-handle) end of the spit first through the centre of the pig from the bottom to the head, entering through the hole underneath the tail, and exiting through the windpipe and mouth. To get the end of the spit through the mouth, prise the jaws apart using a wooden or metal spoon. Adjust so the length of spit is approximately equal at either end.
2. Secure the pig in place on the spit with the fixing skewers. Each skewer should pass through the pig, through one of the holes in the spit, and out through the pig again. The most important one should go through the ribcage and across the middle of the chest cavity. You'll probably get only two others in, one through the neck and one through the lower stomach.

Stage Three: Stuffing and Sewing Up the Pig

Equipment

1 bradawl (a small wood-handled hole-puncher for leather work)

1 sailmaker's needle

thick butcher's string

1 pair of long-nosed pliers

1 sailmaker's glove (optional but very useful)

1 piece of wood, about 60 cm/2 feet long

1. With a small bradawl, make holes about 4 cm/1½ in apart along both sides of the chest cavity stomach opening. They should be about 2 cm/¾ in away from the edge, through the skin and, where possible, the flesh.
2. Using a sailmaker's needle, thick string and a pair of long-nosed pliers, sew up the pig, starting from the beginning of the slit at the top of the throat. Push the needle through the holes made by the bradawl (this is where the sailmaker's glove can come in handy), bringing the two sides of the slit together. A blanket stitch is best (see close-up photograph) or, for less expert seamsters, simple cross-stitch. If you end up improvising your own stitching, just make sure it's good and strong. Use the long-nosed pliers to pick up the point of the needle and pull it through the skin. The stitches should be carefully positioned so that the strain is on the thickest part of the skin, to stop it tearing. If it does tear, make a new hole with the bradawl further from the edge of the skin.
3. The stitching is done in two stages, with the stuffing carried out in between. When you reach the botton of the ribcage/top of the stomach opening, pull the string tight and tie off securely. This first part is the trickiest bit of the stitching.
4. Take the stuffing and fill the chest cavity, going as far up the chest towards the neck as you can. Do not pack the stuffing in too tightly as it will expand in the heat of cooking.
5. Fill the stomach area with stuffing, packing it carefully around the spit inside the cavity. Again, do not overstuff: make sure the two sides of the stomach opening will still come together easily over the stuffing.
6. When all the stuffing is in, begin stitching again, firmly tying the string to the knot made at the end of the ribcage, and carefully sew up the rest of the slit. Make sure that you have not left any gaps, and tie the string tight and very securely at the end of stitching.
7. You also need to secure the feet at either end, so they do not flop about during cooking. To secure the front legs, take a 60 cm/2 foot piece of wood about 2.5 cm/1 in in diameter, such as a thin branch, and tie the two front trotters to either end of it, so they are kept well apart. This will help to ensure that the shoulders get cooked through.
   The back trotters should be tied back towards the spit (not tightly to it, but to within a few centimetres of it). Tie some string around one hind trotter, tie it around the spit (through a hole if one is available), then around the other trotter, keeping the string fairly taut.

Basting the pig before placing it in position over the fire (stage five) ▶

Stage Four: Preparing the Fire

Fred prefers apple or cherry logs for his fire, because they give a good flavour (and extend the fruit/pork connection in a satisfying manner). But you can use almost any well-seasoned (i.e. not freshly cut) wood logs, except pine and yew, as they are liable to impart an acrid taste to the meat.

Equipment

a large load of logs

rake for the fire

1. Make a large fire with plenty of logs between the supports of the spit. Light the fire at least an hour before you want to start roasting the pig.
2. When the wood has burned down to hot embers, after about an hour, rake them away from the centre to make an oval-shaped ring of fire, a little wider and longer than the pig, with the spit supports at either end. This is very important: the pig should not be directly over the fire, or dripping fat will catch fire and burn the pig.
3. Fire maintenance: you will need to keep feeding the fire, a few logs at a time, throughout the cooking. So keep a good woodpile close (but not *too* close) to the fire. You want to maintain an even heat of flickering rather than soaring flames and not get the fire so hot you cannot go near it.

Stage Five: Cooking and Basting

As with the preparation, patience and attention to detail are the keys to successful cooking. Fred says you should always make far more of the baste than you think you'll need because as soon as your guests arrive they will all want to have a go at basting the pig. What's left of the baste will quickly disappear.

Equipment

1 wide paintbrush, attached to a broom handle or long piece of wood

1 bucket

1 large saucepan for baste

meat thermometer (optional)

for the baste

1 litre/1¾ pints sunflower oil

1. Put all the ingredients for the baste into a large saucepan or bowl and mix well. Keep near the fire.
2. Take the pig outside and place on a suitable clean flat surface such as an outdoor table (on which you can also carve and serve the pig).
3. Carefully baste the animal with the very oily vinaigrette baste, using a clean paintbrush attached to a piece of wood. Make sure that all the string is very well soaked with the baste. If the string burns, the animal will explode open and the stuffing will spill: the major catastrophe of the spit-roast.
4. When the whole pig has been thoroughly basted, get a friend to help you take the pig-on-the-spit to the forked supports, carrying it at each end. Place the spit very carefully on the supports, making sure that the octagonal cross-plate by the handle fits neatly into the support. The pig should be roughly centred above the empty middle of the oval fire.
5. Apply more baste liberally and leave to roast slowly. Depending on how hot or cold the day is, the pig will take between 6 and 8 hours to roast. It needs to cook

120 ml/4 fl oz cider vinegar

½ tube of garlic paste

large handful of fresh thyme

1 tbspn Moroccan barbecue spices (optional)

1 tbspn salt

freshly ground black pepper

gradually, turning a darker and darker gold each hour. On a hot day in June, during filming, the pig took about 7½ hours to cook, over the right heat. If the heat is too high, you will get a burnt outside and a raw inside. Undercooking is one of the dangers of a spit-roast. It is better to end up absolutely frazzling the outside to get nicely cooked meat.

6 Make yourself comfortable with a good book and a beer and turn the spit every 5–10 minutes. Keep the pig well basted, and be sure to keep the string basted so it doesn't burn. Keep the fire hot but don't allow the skin to catch or burn; you want the skin to be golden and not black. Check the fire every time you turn the spit. Concentrate on getting an evenish heat, but with the fire slightly hotter near the front and back legs, where the meat is thickest. The legs need the most heat, followed by the shoulders. Use a rake to maintain the correct oval shape of the fire.

7 Towards the end of cooking (the last hour or so), the crackling should develop. If you have too much heat too near the beast, the skin will bubble too early. If the crackling hasn't crisped up properly when the pig is ready, you can make the fire much hotter by throwing on some more logs in the last half-hour of cooking. The flames will quickly crisp up the skin, but watch carefully and turn frequently, as the skin can quickly burn. On the day of his party, Fred got the crackling spot-on around the back and shoulders, but we slightly burned the belly.

Stage Six: Finishing and Serving

1 If you maintain the heat correctly, you can time when the meat should be ready. To check, stick a long knife into the thickest part of the meat. The juices should run clear and the tip of the knife should be hot. Fred uses a meat thermometer and finds that when the temperature at the centre of the meat is right for medium beef, the pig is ready. *Take care not to serve rare pork.*

2 With one person at either end (the person at the head end will need oven gloves to pick up the non-handle end of the spit), carefully take the pig on its spit off the support rods. Put the pig on the carving/serving table on its side. Before you take the spit out of the pig, cut a deep slash, down to the bone, on one of the legs to double-check that it is cooked through. If not, put the pig back over the heat. When you are sure the meat is ready, remove the cross-rods and spit from the pig.

3 Using a sharp knife, cut the stiching down the stomach and carve a couple of half-moons out of the stomach skin so you can get at the stuffing.

4 Get some friends to help carve and serve out the meat, stuffing and crackling so everybody gets the food before it gets cold. Have one person serving stuffing, one on crackling and two or three people carving the meat. To make the carving easier,

they should first remove a leg or a shoulder off the main body and carve the meat from the joint rather than straight off the body. Get your guests to queue up with plates so they get the meat while it is still hot. Make sure that everyone gets some crackling and stuffing.

Three Pepper Salad

serves fifty

10 red peppers
10 yellow peppers
10 orange peppers
10 cloves of garlic, thinly sliced
lots of extra virgin olive oil
salt and freshly ground black pepper
3 handfuls of pine kernels
a fistful of coriander or basil leaves, roughly torn

1. Preheat a grill to high.
2. Deseed and slice the peppers into long strips, 2 cm/¾ in wide.
3. You will probably have to grill in several batches. Put the pepper slices in a shallow casserole dish or baking tray with the sliced garlic, olive oil, salt and pepper.
4. Roast the sliced peppers under the hot grill until they start to blacken round the edges, turning occasionally. Allow to cool.
5. Toast the pine kernels in a dry frying pan, taking care they do not burn. Mix with the peppers.
6. Garnish with the herbs and serve.

Chocolate Brownies

It may seem amazing that Fred's guests still had room for pudding after gorging themselves on the pig and salad, but they made light work of these delicious chocolate brownies.

serves fifty

340 g/12 oz butter
120 g/4 oz cocoa powder
170 g/6 oz plain chocolate
6 medium eggs
a pinch of salt
675 g/1½ lb caster sugar
170 g/6 oz self-raising flour

1. Preheat the oven to 180°C/350°F/Gas mark 4.
2. Melt the butter in a pan over a low heat. Stir in the cocoa powder.
3. Add the chocolate and stir until melted.
4. Put the eggs in a bowl. Add the salt and sugar. Whisk thoroughly and then whisk in the chocolate mixture.
5. Fold the flour into the mixture.
6. Put the brownie dough into one or more buttered baking tins and bake for 40 minutes.

◀ Baste the pig regularly, making sure that the string in particular is kept moist so that it doesn't burn.

LATE STARTER

Wendy Ingham

MENU

Individual onion and goat's cheese tarts with walnut pastry

Chicken with tarragon
Gratin dauphinois
French beans

Chocolate and coffee mousse cakes

Today's top female executives are often too busy to eat, let alone cook. And for many of them the kitchen remains a symbol of domestic drudgery, lack of opportunity and subservience to men – a place they're glad to have escaped from and have no wish to return to.

From her days as a high-flying student, this philosophy was embraced wholeheartedly by Wendy. 'At university, food was just fuel,' she recalled. 'I lived off muesli and battered sausages from the chippy. I couldn't see the point of all that shopping and cooking for something to be eaten in ten minutes.' Wendy took this attitude to food with her into her marriage and career: 'Until a couple of years ago, I hadn't cooked a single dinner party. I'd hardly even cooked for Robert, beyond heating up the odd pizza.'

What little cooking was done at home was done by Robert. If they entertained, he would cook a curry. 'When we went out to dinner with friends,' Robert recalls. 'I don't think Wendy even tasted the food. She certainly never mentioned it.'

So how did such an unfoody come to feature on our show? Because a couple of years ago, on holiday in the South of France, Wendy met Lemmy, and Lemmy was a mad keen cook who ran a cooking school. 'I'd met people like Wendy before,' Lemmy told me. 'Career types who didn't think food was important. And when I was cooking on the first night, I overheard Wendy saying something like, 'Boil in the bag rice is about all I can do.' It wasn't a great start.'

But in fact it was Wendy, not Lemmy, who was in for a shock. 'Something about that place,' she remembered, 'the weather, the people . . . the food. I realized for the first time that eating – really tasting things – could be quite exciting.'

Back in England, Wendy enrolled on one of Lemmy's cooking courses, and the two became great friends. And when Wendy is cooking, Lemmy's word is pretty much law. She still cooks from the recipe sheets Lemmy gave them on the course: 'I feel safe with them.' They have formed the basis of half a dozen dinner parties that Wendy has cooked since she saw the gastronomic light – all of which have gone pretty well. 'Except once,' Wendy admitted, 'when I asked Robert to do some washing up while I went to have my shower. He washed up the meat pan which had all the juices for my sauce. I threw a stamp-foot tantrum. Then after I'd had a good cry,' she confessed in a guilty whisper, 'I used. . . *a stock cube*.' I promised not to tell Lemmy.

Until she cooked for the show Wendy had never invited Lemmy. 'I didn't feel ready,' she told me on the day of the dinner. 'In fact, I'm not sure that I feel ready now!' But in the end, the tart was a triumph, the chicken got top marks, and it was all right on the night – almost.

Wendy had decided, as an extra touch of class on the side of the truffle cake dessert, to paint some little ivy leaves with chocolate and use flowers to decorate the plates. Lemmy, who brings her professional critical faculties with her to the dinner table, did not approve. 'Chocolate decorations and flowers should *always* be edible,' she admonished, with a wag of her finger. 'You can never be sure that someone won't be stupid enough to eat them.'

Well, I'd already licked the chocolate off a couple of them, so I guess she was right about that.

All the recipes for Wendy's dinner were devised by Lemmy, for her cookery school, Cuisine Eclairée, in Yorkshire.

Onion and Goat's Cheese Tart with Walnut Pastry

An inventive version of tart tatin, inspired by the ingredients Lemmy enjoyed when living in the Perigord region of France.

serves six as a starter

50 g/2 oz butter

1 kg/2¼ lb red onions, very thinly sliced

2 tbspn olive oil

100 ml/3½ fl oz white wine

1 tbspn white wine vinegar

1 tspn chopped fresh thyme (or ½ tspn dried)

salt and freshly ground black pepper

300 g/11 oz puff pastry

3–4 tbspn finely chopped walnuts

3 tomatoes, thinly sliced

100 g/4 oz goat's cheese log, finely diced

6 tspn walnut oil

1. Grease six small individual tart dishes with butter.
2. Melt the butter and fry the onions very gently in the butter and olive oil for about 10 minutes, stirring occasionally with a wooden spoon or spatula, until soft and golden (do not allow to burn).
3. Add the wine, vinegar and thyme and cook until all the liquid has evaporated. Season with salt and pepper.
4. Divide the pastry into three, sprinkling each piece with the walnuts, then stack the pieces on top of each other and roll out thinly.
5. Cut six discs of pastry to the size of the tart dishes, then place in the fridge for 30 minutes to rest.
6. Preheat the oven to 220°C/425°F/Gas mark 7.
7. Place a few slices of tomato on the bottom of each dish and then divide the onion mixture between the dishes.
8. Place a disc of pastry over the onion mixture and tuck the edges in. Prick all over with a fork to help to keep the pastry crisp.
9. Place in the middle of the preheated oven for 15 minutes until risen and golden.
10. Remove from oven and put a plate over each tart dish. Invert and shake firmly.
11. Slide each tart on to a greased baking sheet and sprinkle with goat's cheese and the walnut oil. Place under a preheated grill to melt the cheese.
12. To serve, accompany with a crisp salad of baby leaves, sprinkled with a few walnuts and a further drizzle of walnut oil.

Onion and goat's cheese tart with walnut pastry ▶

Parsnip and Ginger Soup

This elegant clear soup is flavoured with a hint of fresh ginger. It makes a nice warming supper, but is certainly unusual enough to serve at a dinner party.

serves four as a starter

1 tbspn olive oil
15 g/½ oz butter
50 g/2 oz parsnips, julienned (cut like matchsticks)
50 g/2 oz carrots, julienned
500 ml/18 fl oz good chicken stock
¼ tspn chopped fresh ginger root
salt and freshly ground black pepper

1. Heat olive oil and butter and sweat the vegetables for just a few minutes. Do not overcook as they should still be crisp.
2. Add the chicken stock and simmer gently for 15 minutes.
3. Add the ginger and simmer for a further 15 minutes.
4. Season with salt and pepper.

Tomato Tart

This wonderful tart comes from Tuscany, where Lemmy has a cookery school in the summer. It is delicious served warm or cold.

serves eight as a starter

200 g/7 oz plain flour
100 g/4 oz butter
pinch of salt
5 tbspn ice-cold water
750 g/1 lb 11 oz ripe fresh tomatoes cut into large pieces or 750 g/1 lb 11 oz drained canned tomatoes
1 celery stalk, roughly chopped
1 carrot, peeled and roughly chopped into small pieces
1 small onion, peeled and finely chopped
1 clove of garlic, chopped
large handful of flat-leaf Italian parsley leaves, chopped
5 large basil leaves, torn into pieces
2 tbspn olive oil
2 tbspn butter
salt and freshly ground pepper

1. Sift the flour into a food processor bowl. Add the butter, salt and 2 tbspn of the water and amalgamate the ingredients (using a pulse button if you have one). Add more water as needed to form a ball of pastry dough. If not using a food processor, mix the pastry together by hand in a mixing bowl. Wrap in clingfilm and refrigerate for 2 hours.
2. Place the tomatoes in a large casserole with all the other chopped vegetables and herbs on the top. Pour over the olive oil and cook for 1 hour on a medium heat without stirring but just shaking the pan to prevent things sticking.
3. Put the contents through a food mill or whiz up in a food processor (but do not over-blend).
4. Add the butter and further reduce the sauce until it is quite thick (about 10 minutes). Season with salt and pepper. Cool completely.

3 extra large or 4 medium eggs

50 g/2 oz freshly grated Parmesan

1 large ripe tomato (optional)

5 Thickly butter a 23 cm/9 in tart dish, preferably one with a loose bottom. Roll out the pastry and line the tart dish. Prick the pastry all over with a fork. Refrigerate for 30 minutes.
6 Preheat the oven to 190°C/375°F/Gas mark 5.
7 Put foil in the pastry case and fill with dried beans or purpose-made clay baking beans. Bake blind for 25 minutes in the preheated oven. Remove the beans and foil covering and bake for a further few minutes until golden. Leave to cool.
8 Beat the eggs and Parmesan into the tomato sauce with a wooden spoon.
9 Pour the filling into the pastry case and, if using, thinly slice the ripe tomato and lay it on top of the filling.
10 Bake for 20 minutes. Allow to cool for 15 minutes before serving.
11 Serve with fresh basil leaves and a side salad.

Lemmy's Tuscan Beans

These soft, garlicky, oily beans are great as a topping for crostini (toasted stale Italian bread trickled with extra virgin olive oil) or as a side dish to accompany meaty winter dishes.

serves six as a side dish

100 g/4 oz dried white haricot beans or cannellini beans

1 small onion, peeled

4 cloves

2 tspn tomato concentrate

salt and freshly ground black pepper

1 bay leaf

a few sage leaves

1 tomato, peeled, diced and deseeded

5 tbspn extra virgin olive oil

1 Soak the beans overnight in cold water. The next day, rinse and place in a pan with enough cold water to cover.
2 Pierce the onion with the cloves and add to the beans with 1 tspn of the tomato concentrate and a little salt and pepper, bay leaf and sage.
3 Bring to the boil and simmer for approximately 2-3 hours until the beans are quite soft. If the water evaporates below the top of the beans, add a little more from a boiling kettle.
4 Remove the bay leaf and cloves and onion, and drain off any excess liquid. Add the diced tomato and the rest of the tomato concentrate. Cook for a further 10 minutes, stirring occasionally so some of the beans get mashed and creamy.
5 To serve, trickle over some good, fruity olive oil.

Chicken with tarragon ▲

Chicken with Tarragon

This classic French dish can also be served cold (reduce the chicken stock by a half and not two-thirds).

serves six

2 chickens (preferably free range and/or corn fed) about 1kg/2¼ lb each, cut into 16 pieces (or 16 breasts, thighs and legs)

salt and freshly ground black pepper

40 g/1½ oz butter

a little oil

1 Season the chicken with the salt and freshly ground black pepper.
2 Heat the butter and the oil in a large frying pan or wide casserole dish and brown the chicken all over.
3 Add the bouquet garni, cover the pan and cook for approximately 30-40 minutes (the breasts can be removed after 20 minutes). Lift the chicken out and keep warm.

bouquet garni (the usual parsley, thyme, celery stalk and bay leaf, plus tarragon stems)

100 ml/3½ fl oz white wine

500 ml/18 fl oz dark chicken stock (see note)

¼ tspn cold butter

½ –1 tbspn chopped tarragon leaves

1 tomato, peeled, seeded and diced

4 Pour off the fat, add the white wine to the juices and scrapings in the pan and boil to reduce almost completely.
5 Add the stock and reduce by two-thirds (or by half if serving cold).
6 Strain the sauce and return it to the pan. Whisk in the cold butter, add the chopped tarragon leaves and the tomato and leave on a very low heat for a few minutes to just warm though the ingredients and bring out their flavour.
7 To serve, spoon the sauce over the chicken. Serve with gratin dauphinois (recipe follows) and green beans.

***Note**: A classic tarragon chicken can be made with veal stock. Lemmy makes a rich dark-gold version of chicken stock as a substitute. Roast the chicken carcass until brown and blacken two onion halves, cut side down, in a dry frying pan. Keep the skins on. Make the chicken stock in the usual way.*

Gratin Dauphinois

serves six as a side dish

2 cloves of garlic

150 g/5 oz butter

1.5 kg/3 lb floury potatoes, peeled, washed and thinly sliced

salt and white pepper

750 ml/1¼ pints double cream (or for a lighter dish, half milk and half cream)

1 Preheat oven to 200°C/400°F/Gas mark 6.
2 Rub an ovenproof dish all over with a garlic clove, then butter generously with half the butter.
3 Season the potatoes well with salt and pepper – be generous as they need plenty of seasoning. Layer the potatoes in the dish.
4 Bring the cream to the boil with the remaining garlic clove, then pour over the potatoes, removing the garlic clove.
5 Dot the surface of the gratin with the remaining butter.
6 Put in the oven and bake for 30-40 minutes at 200°C/400°F/Gas mark 6 for the first 10 minutes, then reduce to 150°C/300°F/Gas mark 2 for the remaining 20-30 minutes. The surface should be brown and the potatoes creamy.
7 The gratin is now ready to serve, but it can be left to cool, refrigerated and kept for up to two days. Individual servings can be stamped out with a pastry cutter, wrapped in foil to keep their shape (but leave the top open) and reheated for 15 minutes in a hot (190°C/375°F/Gas mark 5) oven.

***Note**: If making a lighter dish with half milk and half cream, boil the milk and cream separately to prevent curdling. Pour them separately over the potatoes.*

Oven-Baked Chicken with a Herbed Bread Crust

This dish is a delicious low-fat way of cooking chicken, which remains very moist inside the bread crust. Lemmy says children love it. It can be served hot with a dish of vegetables or cold in lunchboxes or for picnics and parties.

serves six

12 chicken thighs

225 g/8 oz fresh bread, white or brown, ideally slightly stale

¼ onion, finely chopped

2 tspn dried parsley or mixed herbs

80 g/3 oz butter

juice of ½ lemon

flour

salt and freshly ground black pepper

2 beaten eggs

1. Remove the skin from the chicken (it pulls away very easily).
2. Cut the bread into small pieces and chop in a food processor with the onion and parsley to get large crumbs. If you do not have a food processor break the bread into pieces as small as possible and add the chopped onion and parsley. Transfer the breadcrumb mixture in a large mixing bowl.
3. Melt the butter and pour over the breadcrumbs, then add the lemon juice. Stir well to ensure all the bread is coated with the butter and lemon.
4. Place the flour in a bowl and season with salt and pepper.
5. Roll a chicken piece in the flour. Tap it on the side of the bowl to remove any excess flour, then immediately dip into the beaten egg. Finally put the chicken into the breadcrumbs. Using your hands, press the breadcrumbs firmly on to the chicken so it has a thick coating of bread. Place on a lightly greased baking tray. Repeat with all the chicken thighs, then put the baking sheet with the chicken pieces into the fridge for one hour.
6. Preheat the oven to 200°C/400°F/Gas mark 6.
7. Bake the chicken for 40-50 minutes. The crust should be golden brown and crunchy.
8. Serve hot or cold with wedges of lemon.

Note: *You can vary the flavour of the crust by the addition of fresh herbs if you have any in the garden or a pinch of curry powder or paprika. The breadcrumbs can be made in advance and frozen in plastic bags.*

Filet d'Agneau, Sauce Pineau

The sauce with this dish is made with Pineau de Charentes, an aperitif from the Charentes region of France. You can also use a sweet wine or sherry.

serves four

500 g/1 lb 2 oz loin of lamb, boned and rolled (ask your butcher to do this for you)

olive oil

few sprigs of fresh rosemary

salt and freshly ground black pepper

50 ml/2 fl oz Pineau de Charentes, sweet wine or sherry

500 ml/18 fl oz dark chicken stock (see note page 96)

¼ tspn cold butter

1. Preheat the oven to 220°C/425°F/Gas mark 7.
2. Rub the lamb all over with a generous smear of olive oil. Place on a rack in a roasting tin and lay the rosemary on top. Season with salt and pepper.
3. Roast in the preheated oven, 30 minutes for rare, 40 minutes for medium to well done. Leave to rest, wrapped in foil and covered in a towel for at least 30 minutes, so the meat fibres relax and the meat is tender. Save the juices which come out.
4. Pour away only the fat in the roasting tin, then place the tin on a high heat on top of the stove until it smokes slightly. Pour in the Pineau or chosen alchohol and reduce to a syrup scraping up the residue on the bottom of the pan.
5. Add the chicken stock and any juices released by the rested lamb. Reduce by two-thirds.
6. Adjust the seasoning and whisk in the cold butter. Strain and keep warm.
7. Slice the lamb (reheat first in a hot oven for 2 minutes if it has cooled too much) and serve on hot plates surrounded by the sauce.

Chocolate and Coffee Mousse Cakes

The joy of this indulgent dessert is that it is rich with chocolate and cream but still has a light texture.

serves six

for the sponge

2 eggs, separated

50 g/2 oz caster sugar

50 g/2 oz plain flour

40 g/1½ oz butter, melted and left to cool

for the mousse

150 g/5 oz good quality chocolate (at least 55 per cent cocoa solids)

1 tspn strong coffee granules

2 egg yolks

500 ml/18 fl oz double cream, whipped fairly stiffly

1 tspn Cointreau (optional)

10 ml/½ fl oz water

2 tbspn granulated sugar

2 tbspn dark rum

grated chocolate (optional decoration)

finely shredded orange peel (optional decoration)

chocolate-covered coffee beans (optional decoration)

1. Preheat the oven to 170°C/325°F/Gas mark 3.
2. Make the sponge by beating the egg whites until the whisk leaves soft peaks, then add the sugar while beating continually.
3. Whisk in the egg yolks, then carefully fold in the flour.
4. Add the butter and stir gently.
5. Pour the mixture on to a baking sheet lined with greaseproof paper. Spread to approximately 1.5 cm/½ in thick.
6. Cook for 10 minutes, then leave to cool on a wire rack.
7. Break the chocolate into small pieces and place with the coffee in a double boiler or a bowl over a pan of simmering water and melt. Do not allow the water to boil for more than a few seconds before taking it off the heat. Stir the chocolate until it is smooth.
8. Remove from the heat and stir in the egg yolks with a wooden spoon and the Cointreau if using.
9. Stir one-third of the whipped cream into the melted chocolate and then gently fold the chocolate into the rest of the cream.
10. Make a syrup by placing 10 ml/½ fl oz of water into a saucepan and add 2 tbspn sugar. Bring to the boil and simmer until all the sugar has dissolved and the liquid has reduced by half. Add the rum and leave to cool.
11. Place an 8 cm/3 in baking ring over the base and cut a disc. Transfer the disc and ring to a serving plate. Repeat for the five other servings.
12. Brush the sponge disc inside the ring with the syrup, then fill the ring with the mousse mixture, making sure to leave no gaps. Repeat for all the servings. Refrigerate, with the baking rings, until required.
13. Carefully remove the rings and decorate as desired. Suggestions: sprinkle the plate with finely grated dark chocolate and shreds of orange rind, or serve with chocolate-covered coffee beans.

Chocolate and coffe mousse cake ▶

VALENCIAN PAELLA PARTY

Dave Hayward

MENU

Sangria

Red pepper salad
Tomato bread with Spanish ham
Anchovy and black olive toasts

Valencian paella

Dave may live in Tunbridge Wells, but he's not definitely not disgusted. Some of his neighbours might be, though, if they knew that one of his favourite foods was flown in alive from Spain, for slaughter in his own kitchen.

'I like to make it really authentic,' says Dave, coining an adjective that will crop up a lot today, 'and getting the little critters in from Valencia adds just an extra touch of class. They feed on wild rosemary there, and I like to think that makes a difference.'

The 'little critters' in question are snails, an essential ingredient in what Dave calls 'the best party dish of all – so good you don't even need plates to eat it off, just a dozen hungry guests with a fork each'. The dish is paella — 'That's pie-*ay*-ah, not pie-*ell*-a,' Dave insists. Dave has strong views about this dish, and his qualification for cooking it, apart from his natural flair for food, is that he is half Spanish.

Dave has certainly done his paella homework. 'The original paella was made by Valencian peasants,' he explained. 'Rice was brought over to Spain by the Moors in the eighth century, and planted in inland lakes, like the one at Albeferra, near Valencia. The Spanish kicked out the Moors, but they kept on growing the rice. I always try and use Albeferra rice, which I bring back from Spain by the sackful.'

Dave insists that the English perception of paella, laden with prawns and mussels, is a product of the Spanish tourist trade and a travesty of the original. 'The authentic paella is really a dish of the land, not the sea. You threw into it any meat you could get your hands on. For the Valencian peasants this meant snails, of course, rabbit and maybe a duck. Sometimes you might bung in an eel from the water in the rice fields.'

The other thing about paella is it should be big. It's a dish to feed the whole extended family. It should therefore be made outside, in a large pan over an open fire, and not, as Dave put it, 'on some poxy electric ring in a stuffy little kitchen'.

In his back garden Dave has built what would appear to the untutored eye to be a brick barbecue. 'Well, you can use it as a barbecue, but in fact it's an authentic wood-fired outdoor paella stove.' (The good news is that you can probably use *your* barbecue to cook a paella.) The wood is the one thing that Dave admits is not entirely authentic: 'In Valencia they would use wood from the orange groves. But the best I can do here in Kent is to use apple wood.'

It may be fine for the paella, but apple wood is an unfortunate choice for cooks, especially when combined with a swirling south-easterly wind. Dave and I spent much of the afternoon running around the barbecue, being chased by plumes of acrid smoke that seemed determined to get behind the eyes and up the nostrils. The arrival of Dave's mum, Solidad, with a jug of ice-cold sangria was, in the smoky circumstances, something of a life-saver.

But not all of the smoke went up our noses. Its presence was evident in the flavour of a truly excellent paella. My hunch is that in Valencia they've never seen anything so. . . well, authentic.

Cooking with Snails

As a gesture of authenticity, Dave has live snails from Valencia flown in for his paella parties, but you don't have to go to such extreme lengths. You can buy precooked snails tinned, frozen or vac-packed in many good delis and specialist food stores.

Or you can collect your own English garden snails, which, although they may not have had the benefit of Valencian sunshine and a wild rosemary diet, are exactly the same species as those Dave uses (what the French call petit gris*). Collected snails should be kept in a box in a cool dark place and fed for at least three days on a one-item purgative diet: carrots, lettuce or rosemary.*
Or, if you really don't like snails, just add plain rosemary to get some of the flavour of the rosemary-fed snails!
The Spanish like to serve their snails with the bodies out of the shell (though still attached), so they don't have to delve for them with pins. To achieve this, they put all the snails in a pan of cold water so that they come out of their shells. They then put them on a very low heat (with salt rubbed around the edge to deter any attempted escapes) and, as the temperature rises, they eventually 'fall asleep'. They are brought to the boil and then gently simmered for ten minutes until tender, at which point they are ready for further cooking – that is, they can be added to a paella or sautéd in very garlicy butter.

◀ Me, Solidad and Dave watching the Paella bubble

Valencian Paella

The quantities below are designed for Dave's 60 cm/24 in paella pan, so if you don't have one you will need an extra large frying pan or a very wide saucepan. If you are brave, you could attempt to cook two half-size paellas in two separate frying pans. Or use half the ingredients for a smaller paella to feed four. Dave has made his own customized paella barbecue, but a well-stoked conventional barbecue will produce sufficient heat for you to cook yours out of doors.

serves eight

2 tbspn olive oil

250 g/9 oz chicken pieces, in 2-bite chunks

250 g/9 oz rabbit, in 2-bite chunks

250 g/9 oz duck, in 2-bite chunks

250 g/9 oz runner beans or long green beans, cut into 5 cm/2 in slices

½ a green pepper, finely chopped

½ a red pepper, finely chopped

1 large tomato, grated or skinned and chopped

1 tspn paprika

1 clove of garlic, finely chopped

200 g/7 oz butter beans, soaked overnight

450 g/1 lb long-grained rice

1–2 pinches saffron

salt

15–20 snails, prepared as on p.130 (or tinned or vac-packed)

rosemary (optional)

1. Heat the oil in the pan and add all the meat. Fry, turning regularly, for 5 or 10 minutes until all the pieces are nicely browned.
2. Add the runner/green beans and stir-fry for a couple of minutes.
3. Add the diced peppers and stir-fry for a couple of minutes.
4. Add the tomato and garlic and fry for 5 minutes, stirring occasionally.
5. Add the paprika and stir into the mixture to heighten the colour and season the dish.
6. Pour enough cold water to cover the meat and vegetables. (In a paella pan, the tradition is to add water until it comes up to the rivets of the pan.) Ideally the water should be hard, like the water of Valencia, so the water in Kent, where Dave lives, is fine. Simmer for 5 minutes.
7. Add the soaked butter beans and simmer for 10 minutes.
8. Add the rice. In Spain, the rice is poured across the paella pan in the shape of a cross. You have enough when it stands a finger higher than the liquid. Dave has found that a full pint glass just happens to hold the right amount for his pan.
9. Add enough saffron to give the paella a golden hue. Season with plenty of salt.
10. Add the blanched snails, still in their shells and /or a little extra rosemary.
11. Cook, without stirring, until the liquid has boiled away, controlling the heat and repositioning the pan so the paella bubbles evenly. Check the seasoning: an undersalted paella may taste bland. Don't worry if the rice starts to stick to the bottom of the pan as it's meant to – the crispy scrapings from the bottom, known as *socarrat*, are something the guests will fight over!
12. Hand out forks to the guests so that they can eat straight from the paella dish. Alternatively, serve on plates, trying to be fair with the snails and the *socarrat*.

Fideuá

A traditional Spanish dish on the same lines as paella but with pasta instead of rice and fish and shellfish instead of meat. For this and other recipes, including his paella, Dave uses a technique of quickly pulping fresh tomatoes by cutting them in half and grating them coarsely until he is left with just the tomato skin. You can, of course, skin and chop up fresh tomatoes or use tinned chopped tomatoes.

serves six

2 heads and 2 skeletons of white fish such as plaice or cod, plus trimmings from fish and shellfish (including prawn heads and shells)

2 litres /3½ pints water

stock vegetables – small onion, carrot, leek top and parsley stalks, etc.

approximately 450g/1 lb mixed shellfish, such as large prawns, squid and scallops or mussels

olive oil

1 medium onion, finely chopped

1 tomato, grated or skinned and chopped

1 tspn sweet paprika

approximately 450g/1 lb white fish, such as monkfish, John Dory or turbot, ideally in boneless, skinless chunks

400 g/14 oz bucatini pasta (long thin macaroni tubes – if you can't get them use spagetti), broken into 3 cm/1 in lengths

large pinch of saffron

chopped chives

extra trickle of best olive oil

1. To make the fish stock, simmer the bones, fish trimmings and stock vegetables in the water for just 20 minutes. Strain through a fine sieve.
2. Stir-fry the shellfish in olive oil in a paella pan, large frying pan or wok for just a couple of minutes until just cooked. Remove with a slotted spoon and put to one side. If using mussels, remove at least some of the shells.
3. Add the onion to the same pan and fry gently until soft.
4. Add the tomato and paprika and fry gently for 4 minutes.
5. Add the remaining fish and cook for 1 minute.
6. Cover the fish with the stock. Bring back to the boil and add the pasta.
7. Add the saffron to give the fideuá a golden glow.
8. Boil until the pasta has taken up all the stock. (If the pasta is clearly cooked and there is still liquid left, you can cheat by pouring it off!)
9. Return the shellfish to the pan to heat through. Serve in warm bowls with a sprinkling of chopped chives and olive oil trickled on top.

Wild Mushroom Risotto

Dave says the secret of making a good risotto is to keep the stock very hot as you add it, ladle by ladle, to the rice.

serves three–four

- *65–75 g/ 2½–3 oz dried porcini (ceps) mushrooms (optional)*
- *30 g/1 oz butter*
- *1 tbspn olive oil*
- *1 small onion, finely chopped*
- *350 g/12 oz Arborio rice*
- *salt*
- *1 wine glass/100 ml/3 fl oz white wine*
- *1 litre/1¾ pints chicken stock or water*
- *400 g/14 oz fresh cultivated and wild mushrooms, wiped or peeled*
- *a large piece of fresh Parmesan*

1. If using dried porcini, cover in water and soak for 30 minutes. Drain, reserving the mushroom-flavoured liquid. Strain this liquid through several layers of muslin or a coffee filter. Rinse the soaked mushrooms well under a cold tap and chop roughly.
2. Heat the butter and oil in a pan. Add the onion and cook until soft.
3. Add the rice and stir for 1 or 2 minutes so the grains are coated in butter. Season with salt.
4. Add a glass of white wine.
5. Heat the stock to boiling point (adding the mushroom soaking liquid, if you have it, to the stock).
6. In a separate pan, briefly sweat all the mushrooms (including the porcini) in a little butter, to release the juices.
7. Add a ladleful of the stock to the rice, stirring so the rice absorbs it. Add a handful of the mushrooms. Continue to add the stock and mushrooms until the rice has taken up all the liquid and is *al dente*.
8. Serve at once and bring the Parmesan to the table with a cheese grater.

Barbecued Red Pepper Salad

Dave serves this salad and other tapas with a strong sangria (see page 135) while the paella is cooking. To make into a finger-friendly canapé, serve slices of the dressed pepper on grilled bread trickled with olive oil.

serves eight with other tapas

- *4 red peppers*
- *1 large beefsteak tomato*
- *2 very large cloves of garlic, unpeeled*
- *salt*
- *3 tbspn virgin olive oil*
- *2 tbspn wine vinegar*

1. Prepare a barbecue or preheat the oven to 200°C/400°F/Gas mark 6.
2. Barbecue the peppers, tomato and garlic cloves until the skin has blackened all over, or roast them for 30-40 minutes in the oven.
3. Cool the peppers and peel off the skin. Deseed and cut into large slices.
4. Skin the tomato and mash it to a pulp. Squeeze the soft pulp out of the garlic cloves and add to the tomato.
5. Add the oil and vinegar to the tomato and garlic and mix well to make a dressing. Season with salt.
6. Arrange the pepper slices in a serving dish and pour over the dressing.

Tomato Bread with Spanish Ham

A simple Spanish way of flavouring bread is to rub it with a cut tomato and trickle over some olive oil. In this recipe, cured Spanish ham is used as a topping, but another variation would be to top the tomato-smeared bread with slices of piquant chorizo sausage and green olives.

serves eight with other tapas

1 baguette
1–2 ripe tomatoes, halved
olive oil
salt
8 slices cured Spanish ham (Serrano ham is the best)

1. Cut the baguette into thin slices.
2. Rub one side of each slice of bread with the cut side of the tomato.
3. Trickle a little olive oil over each slice of bread and season with salt.
4. Top each slice of bread with a piece of ham.

Anchovy and Black Olive Toasts

serves eight with other tapas

1 baguette
1 clove of garlic, halved
olive oil
1 tin of anchovies
approximately 30 black olives, halved and stoned

1. Preheat the oven to 180°C/350°F/Gas mark 4.
2. Cut the baguette into thin slices.
3. Rub the clove of garlic over each slice of bread and trickle over some olive oil.
4. Put the bread in the oven and toast until lightly golden and crispy
5. Spread a little bit of anchovy on each toast and garnish with black olives.

Valencian paella ▲

Sangria

To make an extra-special sangria, replace the lemonade with sparkling Spanish wine and add two chopped-up peaches, two chopped-up pears and two chopped-up apples.

serves six–eight

- *1 litre/1¾ pints strong red wine*
- *500 ml/18 fl oz lemonade*
- *juice of 1–2 lemons*
- *zest from one lemon (no pith)*
- *2 wine glasses of rum, brandy or gin*
- *sugar to taste*
- *1 stick of cinnamon*
- *ice to serve*

1. Mix all the ingredients except the ice and chill.
2. Serve with plenty of ice.

A NEW ARRIVAL

Gordon Perrier

MENU

No. 5 Special
Canapés

An arranged bouillabaisse

Veal and wild mushroom salad

Gilded pears with goat's cheese

Oranges in Cointreau syrup and sugar cages
Summer pudding
Mango fool
Frosted grapes wtih Marsala cheesecake

Home-made truffles

A man who has spent ninety-six hours of his life putting gold leaf on the ceiling of his bedroom is, you might conclude, a man of opulent tastes who cares about the way things look. In the case of Gordon, anything you can say about his devotion to style and aesthetics is liable to be an understatement.

The decoration, lighting and arrangement of *objets* in the Islington flat he shares with his brother Raymond is a never-ending project that takes up almost all his spare hours. 'I won't allow myself to finish something,' Gordon confessed, 'unless I feel I've done it in the best possible way. . . while other people could spend ten minutes and walk away thinking it was fine, I keep going back and changing things until I'm absolutely happy. I can't allow myself to be surrounded by something that isn't absolutely perfect.'

But there is one other activity that he somehow manages to find time for – entertaining for friends. And as you might expect, Gordon's forays into the kitchen are another extension of his aesthetic mission. 'We like to create very intimate gatherings here,' he explained. 'Part of the inspiration for what we do is the encouragement of our friends, who really appreciate the little details when we're entertaining.

'When I'm cooking, of course, there isn't always so much time. You can't spend an hour arranging a plate, or people would never get to eat anything. So I like to make food that is simple and fresh, and often cooked at the last minute. . . But I'm still very concerned about the way the food looks. I want it to be pleasing – absolutely beautiful if possible – but if it hasn't got the taste, then there's no point.'

The event this dinner was celebrating was special indeed for Gordon – the arrival of a long-awaited item that symbolized his commitment to beauty, to his friends and to entertaining. The piece in question was a round dining table with eight chairs, specially commissioned by Gordon and Raymond, and almost a year in the making.

When the table had been assembled in the space hallowed for it, and the chairs, each upholstered in eight 'summer colours' of velvet, arranged around it, Gordon sat at it for a few moments in awed silence, contemplating the rosy glow of the steamed pear wood. Then he began, with his characteristic quiet and meticulous enthusiasm, to tell me about it.

'It's an incredibly special thing for us – the culmination of a plan to create the perfect environment in which to be with our friends. We always wanted a round table – like Camelot. It's more egalitarian, and we believe it creates a very good feeling, more shared conversation. To have eight very special people around this beautiful table, sharing fantastic food, good wine and warm conversation – I'm sure it's going to be wonderful.'

Gordon had his work cut out, coming up with a six-course menu to match the table for aesthetics, opulence and, of course, taste. But as you will see from the pictures and recipes in this chapter, he rose magnificently to the occasion. Despite almost worryingly high expectations of this dinner, on the night they were met in just about every department. At the end of it all I was left wondering how he could possibly top it at his next extravaganza. 'Oh, I'll think of something,' he told me. And somehow I suspect he will.

No. 5 Special

Gordon's version, numbered after his house, of a gin and sparkling wine cocktail that Americans call a 77 which he drinks outside in his rose garden on warm summer evenings.

serves eight

6 large, unwaxed lemons

150 g/5 oz white sugar, caster or granulated

1.4 litres/2½ pints boiling water

gin, to taste

1 bottle sparkling wine

1. Scrub the lemons in warm water. Zest three of them, taking care to get just the peel and no white pith. Put the zest in a large bowl.
2. Squeeze the juice from all the lemons and add to the zest in the bowl. Stir the sugar into the juice.
3. Pour in the boiling water and stir well, ensuring the sugar is dissolved.
4. Cover and refrigerate the lemonade for several hours, or overnight, until chilled. Take out the peel.
5. Chill eight cocktail glasses. Add lots of ice and then fill three-quarters of the glass with the lemonade. Add a measure of gin to taste and top up with sparkling wine.

An Arranged Bouillabaisse

This is a smart version of the classic French fish soup. Rather than cooking all the fish together, Gordon cooks them lightly, separately, and then arranges the fish and shellfish on the plate by placing the shells on a little creamed potato at the bottom of each soup plate and pouring the soup around them. You can be more or less careful according to your style, but however you do it, the colours will look beautiful and the taste will be summer on a plate. You need to use your fingers to enjoy shellfish, so provide fingerbowls and/or napkins. When Gordon served this at his dinner, he draped some nylon fishing netting across the plate and entitled the dish 'What a catch!'

serves eight

fish trimmings for stock (fresh bones and heads)

1.1 litres/2 pints water

bouquet garni (bay leaf, thyme, parsley stalks and celery)

1 onion, sliced

1 carrot, roughly chopped

16 oysters

450 g /1 lb mussels

1. Make a basic fish stock by putting the fish trimmings in a pan with 570 ml/1 pint of cold water, the bouquet garni, onion and carrots. Bring just to the boil and immediately turn the heat down. Skim the stock, then simmer for 20 minutes. Strain.
2. Open the oysters (for instructions see page 94) and store on a half-shell in the fridge. Discard most of the juice.
3. Preheat the oven to 180°C/350°F/Gas mark 4.
4. Trim the mussels of any beards. Discard any which are cracked or do not close when tapped. Cook the mussels in a little fish stock for a few minutes. Throw away any which do not open. Take all but eight of the mussels out of their shells. Reserve the cooked mussels and their cooking liquor, separately.
5. Heat a tablespoon of olive oil in a large frying pan. Add two of the cloves of garlic,

An arranged bouillabaisse ▶

olive oil

4 cloves of garlic, peeled, left whole but slightly crushed

10 shallots, peeled and roughly chopped

3 cm/1½ cube of ginger, peeled and roughly chopped

½ hot red bird chilli, deseeded

8 x 75 g/3 oz salmon fillets

1 lime

salt and freshly ground black pepper

16 large prawns

16 scallops (or 8 very large ones, sliced in half horizontally)

1 wine glass cognac

1 x 790 g/28 oz jar of ready-made French fish soup (optional, but certainly helps to enrich soup)

30 g/1 oz slightly salted butter

8 tspn creamed potato (optional)

8 half scallop shells (optional decoration)

8 red bird chillies

small handful of dill, roughly chopped

8 basil leaves, roughly torn

8 pieces of brioche or ciabatta

a bowl of aïoli

half the shallots, half the ginger and the half chilli. Lightly fry them for a couple of minutes to flavour the oil, but take care that they do not burn.

6 Turn up the heat and when the oil is smoking hot, quickly sear the salmon fillets on both sides so they take up a little colour. Squeeze the lime on to the fish and remove from the heat.

7 Transfer the salmon fillets to an ovenproof dish, season lightly with salt and freshly ground black pepper and then put in the preheated oven for 5 minutes, until the fish is just done, pink and firm.

8 Meanwhile, remove from the pan any of the ginger, garlic and shallot which have burnt. Add some more oil and two more cloves of garlic to the pan, the rest of the shallots and the rest of the ginger. Heat gently for a couple of minutes. Remove the half chilli. Turn up the heat, add the prawns and cook for around a minute. Add the scallops and cook for around 30 seconds on each side, or until they are just cooked through.

9 Add a glass of cognac. Flame by tipping the pan towards the flame so the heated fumes ignite.

10 To complete the soup, remove the prawns from the pan. Remove the garlic cloves and discard. Deglaze any residue of the cooked fish with a little fish stock, then add the rest of the fish stock, the ready-made fish soup (if you are using it) and the mussel liquor into the pan (or, if your frying pan is not large enough to accommodate all this liquid, transfer to a large saucepan). Boil to reduce by a third. Stir in the butter.

11 Warm eight large soup plates, and divide the soup between the bowls. If you want a very smart soup and are using creamed potato to make the shells sit straight, first put a tablespoon of potato on the bottom of each plate, arrange the fish according to stages 12 and 13 and then pour the soup around them.

12 Add the fish to each soup bowl: two oysters in their half-shells, some mussels (one in its shell) and two scallops (one on a half-shell). Lay the cooked salmon fillet over the top and the prawns to the side, playing with the colours and textures to get the best effect.

13 Lay a whole red chilli over the salmon and dress the plate with dill and basil so the green sets off the pinks and blacks.

14 Serve the soup with warm brioche or ciabatta and spoonfuls of thick aïoli.

Veal and Wild Mushroom Salad

An elaborate warm salad which towers up from the plate, full of contrasting textures, from crispy galettes to soft, truffle-scented potato, lightly cooked wild mushrooms and veal.

serves eight

- *8 medium potatoes, cooked and coarsely grated*
- *salt and ground white pepper*
- *50 g/2 oz butter*
- *250 g/9 oz diced bacon*
- *olive oil*
- *680 g/1½ lb loin of veal*
- *570 ml/1 pint veal stock*
- *100 ml/3½ fl oz red wine*
- *16 tbspn creamed potato*
- *2 tbspn truffle oil*
- *400 g/14 oz prepared, mixed salad*
- *½ tbspn white wine vinegar*
- *3 shallots, sliced*
- *1 clove of garlic*
- *24 fresh morels (optional) and 750 g/1 lb 11 oz other fresh wild mushrooms*
- *8 thin slices of baguette, brushed with hazelnut oil and lightly fried*
- *16 oregano leaves, roughly chopped*

1. Preheat the oven to 190°C/375°F/Gas mark 5.
2. Press the grated potato in a tea-towel to extract all the moisture. Season with a pinch of salt and a generous pinch of pepper.
3. Melt half the butter and mix with the potatoes. Divide into sixteen portions.
4. Lightly oil a baking tray. Place a 7 cm/3 in pastry ring in one corner. Put a portion of the potato mixture into the ring and spread it around, pressing down so it is no more than 6 mm/¼ in thick. Repeat to fill the tray. Brush each with a little more oil.
5. Cook in the oven for 10 minutes, turning after 5 minutes with a palette knife. They are ready when golden brown on each side. Make sixteen galettes in total, in several batches if you have to.
6. Fry the bacon cubes in a little olive oil until browned and crispy, and reserve.
7. Add more olive oil to the pan and heat to a high temperature. Sear the veal by browning it quickly on both sides over a high heat. Put the meat in a baking dish in the preheated oven to cook for 10 minutes (for pinkish veal).
8. Pour the veal stock and red wine into the pan while it is still very hot and stir up the residue left from the meat. Boil the liquid hard to reduce it by half and strain.
9. Rest the cooked veal on a board for 10 minutes, then slice the meat into thin slices.
10. Mix a tablespoon of truffle oil with the creamed potato and season with salt and white pepper.
11. Toss the salad leaves in a tablespoon of truffle oil and the white wine vinegar.
12. Melt the rest of the butter in a frying pan. Add the sliced shallots and a clove of garlic which has been crushed under a knife to release its juices. Throw in the wild mushrooms, cooking the most delicate ones last. Cook for a couple of minutes.
13. To assemble the salad, pipe (or spread with a fork) a generous swirl (approximately 2 tbspn) of warm or room-temperature creamed potato on to each plate. Put some salad leaves on top and then a baguette croûton. Put a galette on top of the bread. Fan out the pieces of veal on top of the galette and then put another galette on top. Place the bacon and wild mushrooms at uneven intervals around each plate and trickle on the reduced veal stock in a thin line, forming an uneven, pointed frame around the plate. Scatter over some chopped oregano leaves.
14. Serve the salad slightly warm or at room temperature with puréed spinach, puréed carrots and roasted shallots glazed with some sugar.

Gilded Pears with Goat's Cheese

This dish was a direct celebration of the arrival of the new table (which is made from pear wood). The gold leaf, a touch of opulence, is edible but does not taste of much! The pears can be gilded in advance, but the goat's cheese should be grilled just before serving, so it is creamy and melted just underneath the breadcrumbs, but still cool and crumbly in the middle.

serves eight

8 ripe dessert pears

8 small sheets transfer gold leaf (23¾ carat)

egg white

4 handfuls of dried white breadcrumbs (slices of stale white bread baked until hard and then pulverized)

1 pinch of ground cumin

1 pinch of ground coriander

2 tbspn poppy seeds

1 egg, beaten

8 small whole goat's cheeses

8 thick slices of ciabatta, brushed with walnut oil

8 sprigs of fresh coriander

4 tbspn hazelnut oil

1. Brush the base of each pear with egg white and leave for a few minutes to become tacky. Press the wax paper on which the gold leaf is mounted on to the base of each pear, with the gold leaf on to the egg white. Holding each pear over a pudding plate, peel off the waxed paper and so the excess leaf floats around the plate. Put each pear on its plate.
2. Preheat a grill to high.
3. Mix the fresh breadcrumbs, cumin, coriander and poppy seeds.
4. Dip each cheese into the beaten egg, coating it all over. Roll in the spiced breadcrumbs. Arrange the eight cheeses on the grill pan.
5. Toast one side of the cheeses under the grill for a couple of minutes, so the breadcrumbs are lightly browned. Turn over the cheeses and repeat.
6. Arrange a toasted goat's cheese, a slice of ciabatta and a sprig of coriander on each plate, next to the pear. Drizzle ½ tablespoon of hazelnut oil around each plate.

◀ Gilded pears with goat's cheese

Oranges in Cointreau Syrup and Sugar Cages

The sugar cages are an elaborate but spectacular technique which Gordon employs only when making this pudding for two or three people. Otherwise, serve the oranges plain, perhaps with some caramel chips.

serves two

50g/2 oz granulated sugar

290 ml/½ pint water

1 tbspn Cointreau

2 oranges

100 g/4 oz dark chocolate

2 tbspn double cream

For the sugar cages

140 g /5 oz granulated sugar

75 ml/3 fl oz water

a little grapeseed oil

1. Make a syrup by dissolving the sugar in water and boiling it fast for 3 minutes. Take off the heat and add the Cointreau.
2. Peel the oranges, taking care to remove all the pith. Remove the base of the fruit so it can sit flat on a plate. Soak overnight in the syrup.
3. Melt the chocolate in a double boiler or put in a bowl in a roasting tin half filled with water. Stir in the cream.
4. Spoon a little chocolate sauce into the centre of each plate and set aside.
5. To make the sugar cages, dissolve the sugar in the water. Turn up the heat and boil the syrup until it turns a caramel-brown colour. Remove from the heat. Working quickly (but being careful not to touch the burning sugar), whisk the sugar syrup with two forks held in one hand, lifting the syrup with the forks so that it cools in the air. After a couple of minutes of whisking, threads of sugar syrup will start to form.
6. As the syrup cools and becomes harder, lift the forks higher and higher above the pan until the syrup is viscous and can flow evenly.
7. Wipe the back of a metal soup ladle with grapeseed oil. Dribble the sugar syrup from a spoon over the back of the ladle, moving it backwards and forwards and around the ladle, changing direction and circling the base to strengthen the cage.
8. Trim the edge of the cage by cutting off any trailing bits of caramel with scissors. Be very careful you do not burn your fingers or let the cage slip off the ladle as it is very fragile at this stage. When it is cold enough to handle, take the cage off the ladle very carefully, using two fingers. Take care not to put any pressure on it.
9. Cool the ladle by running it under cold water and repeat the process to make the second cage, reheating the sugar syrup if it has solidified too much.
10. Put an orange in the centre of the chocolate on each serving plate. Place a sugar basket over each orange.
11. Tap the cage open and eat the orange, spiked with shards of broken caramel, with a dessert knife and fork.

***Note**: These sugar cages are best used within a couple of hours of making because they start to wilt.*

Summer Pudding

serves eight

- *1 loaf of medium-sliced good-quality white bread*
- *2 x 400 g/14 oz pitted black cherries in a heavy syrup*
- *30 g/1 oz caster sugar*
- *170 g/6 oz blueberries*
- *300 g/11 oz tin raspberries in syrup*
- *500 g/1 lb 2 oz strawberries, hulled*
- *icing sugar*
- *290 ml/½ pint double cream*

1. Trim the crusts off the slices of bread and cut a bit of bread off each to get squares.
2. Dip a slice of bread into the syrup from the black cherries and put in the bottom of a 1.2 litre/2 pint pudding basin. Line the sides of the basin with the bread, dipping each slice in cherry syrup as you go. Make sure the slices overlap slightly.
3. Dust the inside of the bread with the caster sugar.
4. Layer up the blueberries, raspberries, black cherries and strawberries inside the bread so that when the pudding is cut you see different layers and colours of fruit. Reserve a little of the fruit, or any which does not fit in the basin, for decoration.
5. Put two or three overlapping slices of juice-soaked bread on top of the fruit. Cover the top of the basin with clingfilm and put on it a plate with a weight on top (a heavy tin will do). Refrigerate overnight. After a few hours, you can top up the deep colour of the pudding by running a knife along the side and putting more fruit syrup in the gap.
6. To serve, run a knife around the basin and turn the pudding out on to a serving plate, gently easing it out with the knife if necessary.
7. Dust with icing sugar and decorate with piped whipped cream and more fruit.

Mango Fool

Gordon says the Alfonsa mangoes which come into season in India in May are the best mangoes in the world. He has enjoyed gluts of mangoes when visiting family and friends in India. 'In India you would eat them simply in the bathtub with a fan blowing a cool breeze from the veranda and the faint sound of hawkers busying themselves on the street outside,' he says. This pudding is another way of enjoying this magnificent fruit, any time of the year.

serves two

- *4 large ripe mangoes*
- *2 tbspn thick double cream*
- *75 g/3 oz caster sugar*
- *¼ bulb stem ginger, roughly chopped*

1. Preheat the oven to 180°C/350°F/Gas mark 4.
2. Cut two mangoes in half and tease out the stone. Take the centre flesh out of each half, leaving a thin layer on the skin. Get as much flesh as possible off the other two mangoes. Cut all the mango flesh into rough cubes.
3. Put the chopped mango in a baking dish, cover with foil and cook in the oven for 25–30 minutes. Remove and leave to cool.
4. When cool, whiz the fruit to a purée in a food processor with the cream, sugar and ginger.
5. Spoon the mixture into the scooped-out skin of the four mango halves. Freeze for half an hour before serving. Put two halves back together to present each mango as a whole fruit.

Frosted Grapes with Marsala Cheesecake

serves two

- *1 large bunch of seedless black grapes*
- *1 egg white, lightly beaten*
- *30 g/1 oz caster sugar*
- *6 digestive biscuits, crushed*
- *30 g/1 oz melted butter*
- *2 tbspn Marsala*
- *200 g/7 oz cream cheese*
- *6 g/¼ oz powdered gelatine*

1. Brush the grapes very lightly with egg white, more on one side of the bunch than the other. Put the caster sugar in a shallow bowl and dip the grapes in it so the sugar sticks to the egg whites. Shake to remove the excess sugar and refrigerate.
2. Mix the crushed digestives with the melted butter. Press into a lightly oiled 7 cm/3 in ring mould on a lightly greased tray.
3. Prepare the gelatine by sprinkling it into a cup of 50 ml/2 fl oz of just-boiled water and stirring until dissolved.
4. Mix the Marsala with the cream cheese and gelatine.
5. Press the mixture into the mould, smoothing the top as much as possible. Refrigerate for a few hours to set.
6. Unmould by running a sharp knife around the edge of the mould. Decorate with the grapes.

Home-made Truffles

At the end of Gordon's dinner, the truffles were served on a draughts board, and the guests had to play draughts, and win a truffle, before they could eat one.

makes roughly twenty

- *200 g/7 oz good-quality chocolate (dark, milk or white)*
- *3 tbspn double cream*
- *2 tbspn liqueur*
- *other flavourings (see below)*

1. Melt the chocolate in a double-boiler, in a bowl in a bain-marie or in a microwave.
2. Heat the cream so it comes just up to the boil, then mix in any liqueur you are using to flavour the truffles.
3. Mix the cream and chocolate together in a food processor or very quickly by hand.
4. Stir in the flavourings you want to use (see below).
5. Refrigerate for about 40 minutes. When the mixture is almost set but still pliable, form balls of the mixture between two teaspoons.
6. If you want, dust the truffles with cocoa powder.
7. Truffles are best kept for a few days to improve the flavour.

Flavourings

Lime and Vodka Truffles: zest of 1 lime, 1 tbspn lime juice, 2 tbspn caster sugar, 2 tbspn vodka. Add more sugar if the taste is too sharp.
Cointreau Truffles: finely grated zest of one orange, 2 tbspn Cointreau.
Whisky Truffles: 2 tbspn whisky. Dust these truffles with cocoa powder.

Summer pudding ▶

A FUTURIST FEAST

Celia Lyttleton

MENU

Futurist cocktails

Cubist canapés

Italian flags

Gilded quail

Bandaged fish

Italian breasts in sunshine

While many of our cooks in the series had all kinds of original ideas about food and entertaining, most of them kept their dinners approximately within the realms of social convention: that is, they sat their guests at tables, started with a starter, ended with a pudding – and gave them a knife and fork to eat with.
But not Celia.

One suspects that Celia was born eccentric – probably wearing a silly hat – and though I've no idea what food was served in her nursery, you can be sure she tried a number of things that weren't on the menu – playdough, pillow feathers, the cat's ear. For now the adult Celia has a roving eclectic eye for unusual culinary items. She tends to cook in faddish phases – for six months it was nothing but Japanese, while at another time she suffered an extended bout of Turkey-mania (the country, not the bird).

But at the time that we caught up with her, she was big into the Futurists. 'A very inspiring bunch,' she described them, 'and way ahead of their time' – as, of course, you'd expect from the name. This group of early-twentieth-century Italian artists and intellectuals set out to celebrate all things new and progressive. They loved machines, especially aeroplanes, cars and any mechanical gizmos and gadgets. As Celia put it, 'They would have died for a Magimix.'

As well as revelling in the new, the Futurists also condemned the torpid traditions that they felt made much of the Italian population 'backward and slothful'. The interminable diet of pasta was thought largely to blame, and in its place they proposed a new and exciting national cuisine.

The Futurist take on food was put into print by the poet and journalist Marinetti, who wrote *The Futurist Cookbook* – a series of recipes, menus and prescriptions for banquets designed to invigorate and excite debate – which is exactly what Celia wanted her dinner to do. 'In a way they invented nouvelle cuisine,' she explained. 'They were into surprising combinations of tastes and colours, often presented very graphically.'

Celia insists that Futurist food isn't just a joke – though it can be pretty funny. For example, not all Futurist 'dishes' are meant to be eaten. And this is where they depart radically from the norms of entertaining. 'A Futurist dinner is a multiply-sensorious experience, if you can say that.' (Celia can say anything she likes.) 'The aim is to engage touch, hearing and sight – and sometimes a little note of eroticism.' The Italian Flags, for example, are served with a 'feely dish' on the side – pieces of sandpaper, velvet and silk, intended to be stroked by the left hand while the right propels the food to the mouth. Not necessarily sexy, but definitely weird.

This was actually the first story we filmed, and I can tell you it was a baptism by fire – literally, at one point, as Celia had left me in charge of numerous kitchen tasks, while she went off to 'lubricate her guests' with a first drink. I left some focaccia for the Italian Flags beneath her very temperamental grill, while I went wash to the spinach. Suddenly the focaccia combusted and flames leapt from the grill.

Having put out the fire, I started again. In retrospect, I'm sure I should have just taken the grill pan to the drawing room, and flung the flaming missiles of focaccia at Celia's recently arrived dinner guests, setting fire to their clothes. I'm sure Marinetti would have approved.

The following recipes of Celia's are inspired by and adapted from The Futurist Cookbook *by Marinetti.*

Futurist Cocktails

The Futurist Cocktail

When mixing drinks, as when cooking, Celia tends not to bother with exact quantities. The measurements given here are a rough guideline. Mix your cocktail according to taste.

serves six

ice

1 litre/1¾ pints freshly squeezed orange or mandarin juice

200 ml/8 fl oz rum

100 ml/4 fl oz strega or campari

1. In a large jug half-filled with ice, mix the orange or mandarin juice with generous quantities of rum and strega or campari. Serve in champagne flutes.

Blue Asti Spumanti with Trapped Beauties

Blue Curaçao, chilled

Asti Spumanti, chilled

For the trapped beauties

water

edible flower petals

summer berries

1. Make the 'trapped beauties' in advance: make ice-cubes as usual, but place tiny flower petals and/or summer berries, or any other amusing items you care to think of, in each.
2. Pour a measure of Blue Curaçao into a large glass jug and fill with Asti Spumanti. Top with a cluster of trapped beauties.

Cubist canapés ▶

Cubist canapés

Celery batons sautéed in olive oil and paprika

artichoke hearts stuffed with sautéed grated carrot and topped with peas

dates stuffed with anchovies

cubes of mozzarella cheese with slivers of pepper arranged diagonally on top

black olives

sliced, trimmed fennel hearts

kumquats with the bottoms sliced off so they sit flat

1 The canapés are laid out in an intriging Cubist pattern on a large rectangle of marble or a sheet of gloss. See the picture on p.151 for Celia's design.

Italian Flag

The Futurists were, of course, passionately patriotic Italians, so it was only natural that Celia would want to fly the flag.

serves six as a starter

2 red peppers

1 tspn honey, heated to make runny

a small pinch of cinnamon

250 g/8 oz bag fresh spinach leaves, thoroughly washed

1 tbspn olive oil

75 ml/3 fl oz crème fraîche

30 g/1 oz walnuts

pinch of nutmeg

1 large loaf focaccia bread

300 g/11 oz mozzarella cheese

6 spring onions or long carrot batons

1. Preheat oven to 190°C/375°F/Gas mark 5.
2. To make the red stripe of the flag, place the whole red peppers on a baking tray. Glaze with honey and sprinkle with cinnamon. Bake for 25–35 minutes, until tender and lightly browned. Leave, covered, to cool. Remove the seeds and peel off the skin. Purée in a food processor or chop very finely with a knife.
3. To make the green stripe, wilt the spinach in olive oil over a medium heat, with a little water in the pan so it doesn't burn. Purée in a food processor with the crème fraîche, walnuts and nutmeg. Or chop the spinach and walnuts finely with a knife or mezzaluna and mix with the crème fraîche and nutmeg.
4. Heat the grill to high.
5. To make the white stripe, slice the focaccia bread into six rectangles. In the middle of each, place a slice of mozzarella cheese, leaving same-size patches on either side. Put under the preheated hot grill until melted, but do not let it brown.
6. To assemble the flag, spoon a stripe of pepper purée and a stripe of spinach purée on either side of the white cheese middle stripe, so each piece of focaccia looks like the Italian flag. Make flag poles out of the spring onions or carrot batons.
7. Serve warm or at room temperature, but do not leave hanging around for long.

Gilded Quail

This highly visual, not to say theatrical, dish was the central 'food happening' of Celia's Futurist feast. The golden quail was flushed out of its cover, shot, plucked, trussed, cooked and served, all within a matter of seconds – apparently! Surprising, then, that it actually tasted rather good, thanks to careful cooking and the unusual but intriguing date and honey stuffing – though I must say I left the silver balls on the side of the plate.

serves six

6 oven-ready quail

for the stuffing

12 dates

½ tbspn grainy mustard

1 tbspn runny honey

lemon juice

salt and freshly ground black pepper

for the 'blood' sauce

a little olive oil

1 large onion

2 or 3 red peppers

a large tin (800 g/28 oz) plum tomatoes

for the gilt glaze

1 egg yolk

1 tspn runny honey

a splash of rum or brandy

1 heaped tspn turmeric

for presentation and serving

silver sugar balls

yellow feathers

a woman dressed as a golden bird

a man brandishing a shotgun

bangers

1. Preheat the oven to 220°C/450°F/Gas mark 7.
2. To make the stuffing: chop the dates roughly with a large knife or mezzaluna. Place in a bowl with a dollop of mustard and a tablespoon of honey. Add a squeeze of lemon, a pinch of salt and a few twists of black pepper. Mix well. The stuffing should be moist but fairly stiff.
3. Using a teaspoon, fill up the cavities of the birds with the stuffing and arrange them on a roasting tin. The birds can be stuffed in advance but should be kept in a cool place until cooking time.
4. To make the sauce: chop the onion and sweat in a medium saucepan in a little oil until soft. Slice and deseed the red peppers and add to the pan. Cook for a few more minutes, then add the tomatoes. Simmer and reduce until soft and pulpy. Liquidize or rub through a sieve.
5. To make the glaze: mix the egg yolk with a teaspoon of honey, a tot of rum or brandy and the turmeric. Stir until emulsified, like thick golden-yellow paint.
6. Put the roasting tin with the birds in at the top of the oven. After 10 minutes, when the birds have begun to brown, take them out and paint on the glaze using a pastry brush. Return to the oven for 5 minutes. Remove from the oven and touch up with the last of the glaze.
7. Pour the red 'blood' sauce over the base of a large white platter, making sure that it is completely covered. Arrange the six quails facing outwards in a circle, with a few wisps of feathers in between. Scatter the silver balls over and around the birds and into the sauce.
8. For the full Futurist effect, the serving of the birds is preceded by a quail hunt. A lady in a gilded bird costume rushes into the dining room, pursued by a hunter with his gun. He chases her around the table and out of the dining room, whereupon several shots are heard (the bangers), followed by the death song of the quail. Then the dish is immediately brought to the table: gilded quails served in a pool of their own 'blood' with the silver shot from the hunter's gun scattered over the dish.

◀ Gilded quail

Bandaged Fish

A curious dish which, after the manner of Futurist feasts, was served not as a course but as a tantalizer. After the elaborate preparation (the fish is stuffed as well as wrapped), the dish was passed around the guests for admiration, then whisked away, never to be seen again. Except, that is, by me. I ate one in the kitchen and found it delicious, though I wouldn't necessarily recommend you serve it on a bed of green jelly!

serves six

1 packet of green jelly

6 strips of Nori seaweed

mirin wine

3 handfuls of pine kernels

a sprig of fresh rosemary

about a dozen seedless white grapes

salt and freshly ground black pepper

6 red mullets, approximately 250 g/8 oz each, gutted and scaled

1. Make up the green jelly according to the packet instructions and put in the fridge to set.
2. Put the strips of seaweed in a pan and cover with a slosh of the mirin wine and enough water to cover. Bring to the boil, then simmer for a few minutes until soft and pliable.
3. Toast the pine kernels in a dry frying pan with the rosemary, taking care not to burn them.
4. Discard the rosemary sprig, then whiz the nuts in a food processor to get a coarse paste.
5. Slice the grapes into slivers. Mix gently with the pine kernel mixture. Season with salt and pepper.
6. Stuff the gutted fish with the pine kernel and grape mixture.
7. Put the fish on a ridged griddle pan or under a hot grill and cook on both sides until done.
8. Wrap a piece of cooked seaweed around each fish.
9. Roughly chop the jelly and spread on a platter or large serving plate to make a 'sea'.
10. Arrange the fish on the jelly.
11. If at a Futurist feast, present these beautiful fish to your hungry guests, then whisk them away again immediately! Otherwise forget the jelly, and serve and eat them as they are.

Further Futurist Ideas

Many highly visual and unusual dishes could, I suspect, be served in the name of Futurism by the imaginative and artistic home cook. Other Futurist-inspired dishes that Celia has served at her dinners, which seem to me worth a whirl, are as follows:

Conquering of the Zenith

Large balls of sticky rice stuffed with wild mushrooms, then coated in breadcrumbs and deep fried. These 'missiles' are served on a 'sea' of avocado purée mixed with whipped cream. Shavings of white truffles scattered over the avocado cream represent white horses in the turbulent sea, and an arrangement of thin strips of lemon rind at the top of the composition are rays of sunshine - and of hope.

City Peppers

Apple slices sweated in butter and flavoured with grappa, wrapped inside a parcel of blanched lettuce leaves and stuffed inside whole red peppers. These are then roasted for 10 minutes in a hot oven.

The Excited Pig

A large skinned salami, pointing skywards at a slight angle, is served with dark honey or molasses. (In the original Futurist version, the salami is served on a pool of cold coffee mixed with a 'a good deal of eau de Cologne'. Celia, wisely I think, chose to omit this detail.)

Equator and North Pole

On a large plate covered with a thin layer of dark red Barolo wine float a dozen lightly poached egg yolks, dusted on top with castor sugar. In the centre towers a cone of meringue, studded with pieces of candied orange, and amongst the egg yolk 'ice islands' float little melon boats, each containing a spoonful of caviar, or some other treasure.

Italian Breasts in Sunshine

A very simple and delicious dessert is created by simply mixing very fresh ricotta cheese with sliced fresh strawberries. I wouldn't hesitate to serve the mixture at a dinner party, though not necessarily in the same way as Celia. She was determined to introduce an erotic note into the proceedings by insisting that guests tackled the breast-shaped mounds without cutlery and with their hands tied behind their backs.

1 kg/2¼ lb very fresh ricotta

450 g/1 lb strawberries, washed, hulled and quartered

1 capful crème de cassis

2 raspberries

runny honey

pink or red rose petals

1. Put the ricotta, strawberries and cassis in a large mixing bowl and mix together very gently, so the cheese retains its fairly stiff texture.
2. Divide the mixture into two equal mounds on a large serving plate and, using a spatula or wide knife, mould them into smooth mounds – 'as high and proud as you can make them,' according to Celia.
3. When you are satisfied with your breasts, take the two raspberries, dip them in honey and put one on top of each mound.
4. Just before serving, scatter fresh rose petals all around the breasts.